Using *Heavenly Faith* to Accomplish EARTHLY GOALS

Using *Heavenly Faith* to Accomplish EARTHLY GOALS

By

John Earl Harris

LOWBAR
PUBLISHING COMPANY

905 South Douglas Avenue • Nashville, Tennessee 37204
Phone: 615-972-2842
E-mail: Lowbarpublishingcompany@gmail.com
Web site: www.Lowbarbookstore.com

Copyright © 2015 John Earl Harris

No part of this book may be reproduced or transmitted in any form or by a means; graphic, electronic, or mechanical, including photocopying, recording, taping, or by any information storage retrieval system, without the prior written permission of the publisher or the author. Poems written by Cal C. Barlow, Junior are used with permission.

Lowbar Publishing Company
905 S. Douglas Ave.
Nashville, Tennessee 37204
615-972-2842
Lowbarpublishingcompany@gmail.com
www.Lowbarbookstore.com

Scripture references in this book are taken from the King James Version (KJV) of the *Holy Bible* unless otherwise noted.

Printed in the United States of America

ISBN: 978-0-9969432-0-8

Manuscript Compilation: Tina Harris
Typist: Tina Harris and Calvin C. Barlow, Jr.
Content Editor: Calvin C. Barlow, Jr.
Editor: Jessica Writer
Cover and Layout Design: Norah S. Branch

For additional information or how to contact the author for workshops or seminars, please contact the publisher.

CONTENTS

Acknowledgement		vi
Chapter 1	The Man	1
Chapter 2	My Vision	5
Chapter 3	Knowledge and Understanding	16
Chapter 4	Faith	22
Chapter 5	Trust, Understanding, and Obedience	28
Chapter 6	Love	31
Chapter 7	The Importance of Attitude	35
Chapter 8	The Importance of People	37
Chapter 9	The Importance of Education	45
Chapter 10	Expressions of Thanksgivings	49
Chapter 11	Conclusion	49
Appendix 1	Newspaper Articles	58
Appendix 2	Messages Excerpts by: John Earl Harris	63
Appendix 3	Revelations	86

Acknowledgements

I am most thankful to God for not giving up on me. It is because of Him this book came forth at a time like this. For a person with limited abilities, I had to live my life by faith and revelations from God. God showed me the completion of this book. He did not tell who would help me, but he told me to say to the people of my community that I would write a book. On December 31, 2003, a lady at H&B wrote down some of my thoughts for this book. I am grateful to everybody who helped me along the way.

Special thanks to Tina Harris! I am grateful to her for typing the first draft of this manuscript. Finally, I am thankful for the belief of my son, Calvin Harris, who had faith in this project and worked tirelessly to see it to completion. Calvin met another Calvin by divine providence in Louisville, Kentucky in the month of February, 2015; because of that meeting, this vision was realized. Therefore, I am very grateful to Bishop Calvin C. Barlow, Jr., writer and publisher of Lowbar Publishing Company for his editorial skills as he gave shape to my story.

Chapter 1

The Man

My name is John Earl Harris; some people call me Evangelist Harris. I am an uneducated man who cannot read or write. In 1956, I married Minnie Bell Hudgins and we had nine children: Minnie Lee Harris, Johnny Lee Harris, Sammie Lee Harris, Johnny William Harris, Ruby Ann Harris, Calvin Harris, Annie Mae Harris, Sylvester Harris, and Stoney Harris.

My father's name was Johnny Harris, Velma Harris was my mother, and Grandpa Sam Harris was my granddaddy. He owned a plantation in Aliceville, Alabama, he was the first person in the county to buy a car and he was not allowed to take it off the train when it arrived. I don't know where my ancestors came from and how they got here. My family had properties taken away from us as much as three hundred acres of land because there were many things we did not know about, so we couldn't get it back. My father and grandfather did all they could to keep the family together. We worked from sun up to sun down out in the fields, it's a lot different today from the way things were back then. We did not have a lot of advantages as we have today, our children and their children don't have to go through such hard times.

The older generations understood the purpose of buying properties. They bought land and left as a family heritage that must not be sold. That was how they were able to hand down properties from one generation to the next. They understood that their children's survival depended upon their wisdom. I have learned that wisdom does not depend on learned knowledge; therefore, it pays to observe others as they make decisions. This is not to dismiss education because life could be difficult without proper knowledge.

The Harris family needs to know we had properties taken from us. Unfortunately, the Harris family was not the only family that was abused in the yesterdays of slavery and Jim Crowism. Today, it's a lot different from the way it was back then; our children and their children don't have to experience the hardship we went through. Things are so much better now, but for some reasons, our children are not taking advantage of these present opportunities. They can get an education, go to college or a vocational school, or join the military. Even though I didn't get an education, there are days that I think about what I missed.

Today, children don't have a slave master over them; however, there are no easy roads to travel. Anything worth having requires hard work. When we work hard for something, it increases our appreciation of that thing. Today, children can be anything they want to be, however, we must put God first in whatever we want to do. Knowing God, staying in touch with Him, and never straying away from his word will make life easier.

Even though I cannot write, others have helped me to make notes of these events. I want my family members to know about the Harris' heritage, our history. I believe that it is important for families to know their origin. Older family members should be wise enough to tell the younger ones about their family, even if there are some unpleasant events in the family history; children need to know their family tree. It's important that each generation pass onto the next generation the family history. Perhaps, if our youths know their family history, it might help them in avoiding some family curses.

It took me over thirty years to get my story into a book; had I listened to my teachers, my journey would have been easier. Before the advent of personal computers, God had shown me how they would be used in our society. Therefore, if you know someone who had dropped out of school, do them a favor by encouraging them to go back to school. Age is no longer a factor; it's not even an excuse. Today there are educational opportunities for the young and the old. Fortunately, in today's society, learning is easily accessible to those who seek it. It is said that a wise man will take instructions, but a fool will not take advice from anyone. When I was young, I was a fool. I am not ashamed to call myself a fool because I am happy God has given me an opportunity to share my failures with others in the hope that they will not make the same mistakes I made.

God gave me the knowledge to know what dope and cocaine can do to an individual. It will destroy the brain cells and hinder the thought process. This is the reason one needs to be careful about the use of drugs. Some drugs are permitted to treat sicknesses, but they should never be used for the purpose of getting *high*. Wise people will take heed and avoid taking illegal drugs. Many older people who have experienced the devastating effects of drugs are trying their best to warn the youths of our society; experience gives you the grace to share with others. God gives directions to people with experience so as to know what to speak about and expect, as physical health and mental health help one to enjoy life. Thus, do all you can do to avoid illegal drugs and other hard substances.

Living the Life

Controlling other people's lives
Is not a leader's trait;
It's serving other people's needs
That God considers great.

Let us think about the good
What's right and pure and true;
May God's word control our thoughts
In everything we do.

The word is filled with so much good
That brings us joy and pleasure,
But true fulfillment only comes
When Christ we love and treasure.

What shall I give you, Master?
You have redeemed my soul;
My gift is small but it is my all
Surrendered to your control.

Not what we have, but we give,
Not what we see, but how we live
These are things that build and bless,
That leads to human happiness.

Chapter 2

My Visions

It started in 1981; I thought it was just an imagination at the time. I had the dream again in 1983 about writing a book. When I told people about it, they laughed at me, nevertheless, I acted. As my book becomes a reality, I wonder what the doubters will say. The writing of this book has been a journey of faith. I have been walking by faith since 1983.

God gave me a revelation about writing a book, and then he showed me the mystery, and I understood it. While I was walking by faith, I did not know what to expect, I thought I was losing my mind as so many things were running through my mind. I found out that it was the Lord talking to me; He wanted me to live by faith. People need to take heed because the Lord has a way of speaking to every individual. If you don't pay attention to God, you will miss out on your blessings. I noted the call and I was blessed. If you are not living a life of faith, the voice of God will confuse you.

When you submit to the Lord, He will reveal things unto you. Faith is simply a mystery. For years, I thought I had faith. I found out that faith is something that increases as we hear and submit to God's word. As we live our lives, we will be tested by our faith.

I have experienced so many things. When I started walking by faith, I discovered the friends I thought I had were not my friends. They thought I was crazy. That was when I realized it had got to a stage where I needed to be all alone. The loss of my friends had me wondering if I should give up on living. Some of them died along the line while others walked away because they misunderstood me. I became sad, and I wrote a song for self-encouragement. These are the words of the song I sang when my friends and loved ones abandoned me: "Jesus was there all the time; he will take me through the storm of life." Those words can encourage you too when people you love walk away from you and say "I don't want you anymore."

In 1983, I started having visions. The Lord spoke to me "use what you have". I was standing on a shovel I had used for eleven years to make a living. Then I had another vision, the Lord showed me what people were going to do to me. He also showed me many snakes; I saw a snake and showed someone else the snake. After I showed that person the snake, there were many snakes and they chased me. In the vision, God showed me the nature of the snakes. Thus, I ran and came to a wired fence. When I tried to go under the wired fence, there was a white dog waiting there. I ran until I got to another fence. I got under that fence, and there was a black dog but the dog did not attempt to bite me.

Years went by, and God showed me another vision. He carried me to a mountain top. While I was on the mountain top, a vision came to me about collard greens. In 1994, I grew collard greens. God shows people things that are to come to pass, yet most people don't pay attention to dreams and visions. There are many stories in the Bible where God warned people before destruction came upon them.

As I have stated, the visions started around 1983. When I started to tell people about my visions, they thought I was crazy because I did not understand visions and dreams at the time; I wanted to tell them how I wasted years of my life by not listening to God. I wanted to save them from the possibility of needless destruction.

God showed me fields of sweet potatoes and collards, and I did as the Lord showed me. He told me to "use what I had"; all I had was just a shovel and a hoe. I had never used a shovel and a hoe for this type of field work. For fourteen years, I used a shovel and a hoe to grow sweet potatoes and collards.

People thought I was losing my mind when I told them what the Lord had shown me; as people talked, I started to doubt. At times, I thought it was my imagination, and every time I was about to give up, something always come to my mind, assuring me it would come to pass. God spoke to me, "It will be as I have shown you". I told people what God was going to do, they laughed because they thought I was a lunatic. I told them it wasn't my imagination and they will see it come to pass. I didn't give up, I kept working with what I had even though people often mocked me; "Where is your trailer home that God is going to give to you?" they often asked.

I have worked an average of four acres per year for a period of fourteen years by faith; I pulled and pushed the wheelbarrow for three years by faith. I lived without the companionship of a wife for twenty years by faith. I lived without a decent home; I didn't have running water, a bathroom, or a bathtub, yet I was convinced that God would restore all these unto me, vindicate me, and people will know what **John Papa** had said had come to pass.

I went into community singing and children started calling me "The Sanctified Man". It was the period when my wife and I separated; people were trying to find out what was going on in my life. They laughed at me as they said, "he is preaching because he lost his family." They thought I had lost my mind. Yet, God was showing me how He could use a person who couldn't read or write in the ministry. It is important to know whose you are and your purpose to others and yourself. Each individual is very important; we all have to learn how to accept the things we cannot change.

God has brought my revelation about writing a book to pass and those that are living will see it. All the things I said had come to pass, even the sweet potatoes' prediction. For the doubters, I made a video of my predictions that have come to pass. I am a believer that you should use what you have; if you have education, use it. God gives men and women gifts and talents to be used to make life better for themselves and others. The completion of this book will encourage people to trust God in matters they might not have complete understanding.

God told me he would make me a man among men. Not above anyone, but he would recognize me because of my faith in using what seemed to be little to produce a great harvest. You see, a lot of people have a lot of properties, money, and education, but they won't use any of it to glorify God and they have doubts in their mind. All things are possible if you have enough faith to believe in what you are doing. God will make it possible because he said "All things are possible if ye believe." This is why faith is important, yet we don't have the same measure. Therefore, we have to be careful not to destroy people as we seek to get them to increase their faith.

Everybody is special in the sight of God and He can use anybody if such will only listen to His voice. I could say this authoritatively because I am a living witness. I wouldn't have been able to tell this story if I had not trusted God. I am a living witness that everybody can do something, no one can say he/she can't do anything because God gave everybody something to do.

I was shy as a child, I didn't appreciate anything people did or said to me. It is my intent to help others not to make the same mistakes I made. Trusting others is a requisite for growth and development. I wouldn't listen to my teachers or my parents. This is why I had a hard time coming up as a child; I had an "I don't care attitude". Learning to trust your teachers and parents will allow you to have a fruitful childhood. You need to take instructions from your mother and father even though you may think they are harsh sometimes, they are preparing you for a world that is often unforgiving.

Life is a mystery, and because of this a lot of younger people get themselves in so much trouble today. They don't listen to anyone; they think that they know more than those who have gone before them. Many of today's youth find it difficult to listen to words of wisdom. It is wisdom that is trying to save our youths from a life of addiction and immorality.

It is my goal to use my wisdom and understanding to help others avoid the pitfalls of life. This book will help someone who doesn't know what life is about. Life is all about being happy, loving, truthful to one's self, and being kind. When you get to a certain age, your thoughts will not be the same as when you were a child or a teenager. Life is what you make of it.

I am using what I have to help others so they won't make the same mistakes I made. I didn't obey those that had more experiences than me. I learnt by my mistakes, it's my hope that others won't have to learn the hard way as I did. If you obey and listen to the wisdom of elders, you might be able to avoid some unnecessary pains of life. As for me, I had no choice but to suffer the unnecessary pains of life because of my disobedience and lack of education.

Life is difficult when you cannot read and write as you have to depend on others in order to do the simple things of life. Not being able to read or write can cripple a family. Oftentimes, those who cannot read and write use drugs and alcohol to enhance their manhood. If you take time to listen to those that have been drug addicts, you will understand how it destroys the family. Many people have died and suffered all because they thought they could find peace of mind in using drugs. The truth is that living on hard drugs will only help one evade or escape the reality of life temporarily. Besides, it is detrimental to one's health.

I have never been a drug addict, but I have a revelation that "drugs will destroy the minds and hearts of those who use them." I hope that everyone who reads this book will think about themselves and others before using drugs. Life is more valuable than we often think.

It took me about forty years to find out what life was about. Every time I sit to talk to different people, I am concerned about how I treat them. Everybody is somebody, and it is important how we treat one another because we need the help of one another. As the years went by, I realized all the opportunities I missed by not following the advice of older people. I really appreciate everyone that has helped me. When someone wants to help you, don't reject it. Understanding the intent of help is paramount. Helping someone understand dope will damage his/her future, helps the person and society. At the time of using dope, most people think they are helping themselves. The same is true of cigarettes – people read the warning on the pack and know how much damage smoking can cause, yet they go ahead and smoke. I bless God as I smoked for twenty years, but I didn't have cancer. We need to heed to all these warnings. This is the revelation that came to me to tell everybody "if they love themselves, they won't put these things into their body system." We've seen and heard how the influence of dope makes people go into a school house, kill their best friends, and not being aware of their actions. Who tells you that you need anything called *influencer* to achieve success in life? Your body is precious, so is your mind. Don't make attempts to destroy them. I believe this revelation will help someone know the truth.

I found life to be sweet when I came to know and acknowledge that God can use anybody. I came to the conclusion that everybody needs somebody to love. I discovered that, sometimes older people would give up on life when they have no one to love. In some instances, their loved ones acted like they did not care about them. This is why when you get to a certain age, your life needs to be a reflection of doing good toward others like your mother, father, brothers, and sisters. When you have done all you know how to do, it will be a help to someone else. This is why you need to use your knowledge and talent because it can help someone else. Everyone should live a good life where somebody can speak well of them.

I have learned through my disappointments how to enjoy life at an old age. One of my purposes for sharing my revelations is to help others. I knew God would make me a man among men, not to be above other men but to show that God can use anybody that will obey Him. Make sure that you go to school. Getting the proper education will help you to express yourself. Knowing how to communicate with other people is crucial, and remember, the lack of education may cause others to make fun of you.

It is necessary to obey your mother, father, and anyone else that is older than you; when you are grown, you will be able to enjoy life. They will tell you what is right because they have already experienced life. It is important you get all the education you can while you are young. You will enjoy life as you will be able to explain yourself to others, and people will not look at you in funny ways. Education allows others to recognize you, and everybody likes to be recognized. However, remember that your attitude makes the difference; knowledge without application and manners is not good enough. Your attitude and the way you treat others make a difference. I have found all this to be true because when I was a child, my unappreciative attitude kept me from getting the necessary education. At the time, I thought people were picking on me, but I found out now that they were only trying to help me. Life can be miserable if you don't do what you are supposed to do while you are young.

I had a vision of how I would be rejected and talked about. I thought I was just an imagination, but I found out that it was God who had shown me these things. As I told people about different things, they thought it was just mere words. I had been at a point when I thought the same thing, but my understanding of the visions became clearer as I walked by faith.

God showed me a lady was going to use me for what she could get. She told me she was in love with me, when I told her what was going on; she didn't believe I was telling the truth. I told the lady what she would need to endure my presence as anyone that is connected with me would be made fun of or talked about. Certain people didn't want other people to communicate with me because they were afraid of the truth. I didn't understand myself and what was happening to me; sometimes I needed to be alone so I could get the answers I needed from the Lord. They thought I was crazy, and they didn't want anyone to talk with me. Some people thought I was selfish, they also didn't know what was going on, but every time someone was in my presence for too long, strange thoughts entered their minds.

I obeyed the vision and planted seeds as I got them. On some occasions, I bought one dollar seeds, and I planted them. I sold some things, took the money and bought more seeds. Sometimes, I would buy fertilizer. People came to me and told me how stupid I was, some people came to me and asked "Have you lost your mind?" By faith, I walked to my job to do the work to the glory of the Lord. There were moments when I thought I had made the wrong choice. After years went by, I understood what the Lord was telling me and I planted more seeds. I had to gather my harvest, but I had no equipment. I borrowed a wheelbarrow for about three months, after which I was able to buy one. Sometimes, I had to push it for a quarter of a mile. People laughed at me as they saw me pushing a wheelbarrow up and down the highway. They didn't know what I was trying to do. I was trying not to be a burden to anyone. The Lord had a mystery in store for me; one of which was good health. People often tell me, "you're in good health', and until this day, I haven't been to a doctor in twenty-three years. A healthy person should be able to encourage others about healthy activities. I discovered that it was a blessing to be able to do what I was doing with the wheelbarrow. Anyone that is able to push a wheelbarrow three, four, or five miles per day, and then walk four miles to Reform, Alabama, is blessed by God. Any man who is also able to get around and enjoy life and do as much as I did at the age of 62 is blessed, not to boast, I give praise and honor to God for sustaining my health.

I use my health and talents to help others. When we use our health and skills to help others (regardless of age, gender, or nationality) God will honor and bless our deeds. One of the greatest honors is to be able to help someone discover the fullness of life.

I was the first deacon of Reform Temple and God gave me a vision about the spiritual growth of the church. I told the people what would happen and they didn't believe it but laughed. I told Elder Hood about the vision, but he thought it was my imagination, and I thought so too. I decided to record my vision because people thought I was a lunatic, I told them the preacher, Elder Hood, was going to leave the church. However, in my vision Elder Hood did not leave Reform and this came to pass. He left the church and started another church in Reform, Alabama. I had told Elder Hood what would happen, but every time I told him, he laughed. He thought that I didn't know what I was talking about. God had instructed me to speak, and I speak whatever He shows me.

I was the first to be called into Gospel Ministry at Reform Temple Church. I had a truck I used to haul wood to the church. The house we met in the church was ragged, and people would come by and make fun of the house. However, God had a lady, by the name, Mrs. Robertson to visit our church; she was a missionary and God had given her a vision about establishing a church.

Mrs. Roberston always attended the church missionary meetings where she tells people how they should live. At that time, I was a drunkard, and she kept preaching to me about the error of my ways. That was a low point in my life; my family would disown me at a time. Often, I was dehumanized while in my drunken moments. However, when she saw I wasn't changing my ways, she talked to my wife. This was before my wife and I separated. Pastor Hudgins also encouraged me to change my habits. I didn't know how, but one day, I turned and gave my life to God. I joined the church, and I became the first gospel minister there, and more ministers were called into Gospel ministry after me.

After I became a minister, another minister invited me to join the Jailhouse Ministry; I thought it was a good thing to continue when the minister left. The inmates had gotten to a place where they thought there was no more hope for them in life. I also helped another minister in Hughes Town whose name is Mr. Guyton. God gave me a vision of helping him. I continued to minister to the inmates, and God showed me a vision of Hughes Temple. I saw what God wanted me to do, He wanted me to help.

I started going to Hughes Town because God had shown me a vision. At the time, I really didn't understand all the details of the vision. As the years went by, the Lord revealed more to me about the assignment; He wanted me to establish a church in Hughes Town, although He didn't want me to be a pastor. He gave that assignment to another man. It wasn't named Hughes Temple; they called it Rose of Sharon. The Lord showed me the people thought I couldn't lead then since I didn't have an education. Yet, I believed God can use anyone for His work; it is important to know what you are supposed to do for Christ. I had told the people my vision, and they looked at me in a funny way. I also told them that one day they would be able to read about the vision for themselves. Once again, I came to the conclusion that my vision wasn't an imagination. Most times, I struggled so hard to be obedient to my vision because I thought it was just my imagination. It is important for every individual to be obedient to the word of God.

I left Rose of Sharon and went to help Bishop Pruitt. I worked with him for a good while, and God showed me another vision of how Bishop Pruitt walked away from the church. God showed me a vision of Reform Temple, the Pastor of Reform Temple, and who would walk away from the church where Bishop Pruitt was the previous pastor. They laughed at me because they thought God couldn't use an unlearned man.

Sometimes after the vision, I helped Bishop Pruitt start a church in Poplar Spring, Alabama. When I told him about these things, he said, "God told him to build a church." Bishop Pruitt went and purchased a building for a church in Reform, then something came up, and he got rid of that church, and Elder Hutton purchased the church from Bishop Pruitt, this is what I had seen in the vision.

God can use a man who has no education; He can use anybody. You have to carry yourself in a way to be used by God. Some people can't be used because they have too much pride in their life, as they are wondering what the next person is going to say or think about them. I came to this conclusion that I wouldn't worry about what people think or say about me. I know that I have to stand before God, and He is not going to ask me anything about anyone else. People need to learn to be themselves everywhere they go. Most of all, love and kindness will speak for itself. It is important to be lovely and kind. I remember a time when I was not kind, but I learned that kindness will take you wherever you need to go even when you don't have a formal education; somebody will see your love and kindness, and give you a helping hand. This has been my experience. Where my education could not take me, love and kindness did. This is a truth that the world needs to know.

Chapter 3

Knowledge and Understanding

This is what the Lord revealed to me: knowledge and understanding. My knowledge and understanding come from the Lord. It is important and wise to listen to those who demonstrate the knowledge of God.

When I was a child, I was given the name "Lolhammer." My teachers tried their best for me to learn but it was difficult for me to understand. Since I could not learn quickly, my teachers fussed at me. I went through life not knowing what my teachers tried to teach me. I really thought they were against me, but they attempted to help me. They were concerned, but I didn't understand them and they didn't understand me. This is what made it a mystery; I was as confused as they were.

After I had grown up, I realized my teachers tried to help me, this is the reason I want to help other students learn from my misfortune. I have experienced how hard it is to help difficult people, it's not a mystery. When people don't understand one another, communication is difficult. Now that

I am older, I realized what life is all about. It took me forty years to understand life; life is a mystery when people don't understand themselves.

God gave everyone at least a gift, every gift has its purpose, and no one can claim superiority because of his or her gift. I grew and matured before I realized my gift had a purpose. Once I had learned what life was all about, my faith began to increase and I was able to enjoy life. Therefore, treasure your gift and use it to God's glory.

Before I could understand what was going on, I had a family: ten children, but one died. My wife's name was Minnie Bell Hudgins. I tried to do what was right, but a lot of the times I was confused and I didn't know how to manage myself. My wife and I didn't have formal education, this made it difficult for us to help our children with their school work. We could not handle the necessity of our family when it came to reading, writing, and understanding each other. The situation got worse and we separated.

After that, the Lord called me into ministry. When I told a preacher God had called me into ministry, he laughed because I didn't have any education, and I was asked questions such as "How do you know God has called you to preach?" However, the children in the church started asking me funny questions; "Do you have some candy?" and call me the "Sanctified Man." They looked down on me because I had a bunch of hogs that I hauled Kudzu (Grass) for; I was called "Kudzu (Grass) Man." or the "Digging Man" because I worked with a shovel. I told them that the Lord had said to me to use what I had and they thought I had lost my mind. When they saw me with that shovel and hoe, they tried to keep me from digging.

The Church of Stansel bought me a garden plow, and I was featured in the newspaper as I work with the shovel and hoe I had worked with by faith. I told a friend of mine whose name is Ben that I wanted him to take some pictures and make a video of my field which we sent to the news agency. Once the newspaper printed my story, some people who knew me got busy trying to stop me from doing what God had told me to do; they started putting metal wires, trucks and cars across the road to keep me from going in and out of my field and on the road so I would have to ask them to let me through. I was trying to let everyone know what God gave me as I made every effort to exercise my faith. Faith without work is dead; I wanted those people to see that "Papa", "The Preacher Man," and "The Vegetable Man" had faith in God. These were some names people called me. Yes, they laughed and mocked me, but I did not let their words stop me from pursuing God's purpose for my life.

I went to several churches, and I was mocked. However, The Church of God in Reform, Alabama was kind – they gave me a tape player and Bible tapes. After a while, I started to purchase Bible tapes for the nursing home ministry in Reform, I had been going there for a long time. I was the first black man to preach to the people at the nursing home, after they had one service, the Church of God helped me hold another service in the nursing home, and whites and blacks started coming to services there. Afterwards, I started a program on the radio station in Gordo. I always made sure that the nursing home received a tape of the message recorded at the station. I will always appreciate the Church of God in Reform for their commitment to God and the way they treated me.

I am not seeking credit for all the Lord has been able to do through me. I only want people to understand we can really help one another. I was raised about three miles from Reform, Alabama, and I try my best to help school children because I don't want them to end up like I did. It is hard to get a decent job and take care of your family without education. This is my message to our youth. It is about being obedient to your mother, father, and teachers. It is especially important to respect your teachers. It is important to have teachers that are really concerned about educating students. It's a mystery to me as some parents fail to work with the teachers and principals; this is a tool for destroying future generations.

God has given each of us different responsibilities in life; it's important to honor and respect other people's assignments in life. The failure to honor and respect other people's purpose in life has caused problems in our society. In some instances, women neglect their responsibilities and try to do what men ought to be doing. God said that the husband is the head of the family; when men fail to obey God's commandment, families suffer. However, when we honor God's word, He is pleased.

God made man in His own image. He took a rib from man and fashioned woman as a helpmeet for him. He gave the man and women an assignment; He told them to be fruitful and multiply. He wanted them to love, honor and respect each other. Yet, love has waxed cold in the hearts of men and women; this is another mystery of life.

There was a time when people loved one another and children had respect for their parents. If only we could learn from the generations that had gone before us, this world would be a better place. If children knew how important their mothers and fathers were, we would not have so much violence among teenagers. I didn't learn the importance of parental wisdom until my parents died. My father tried to tell me something I needed to know, but I didn't take heed until he died. Children should show love to their parents because parents suffer to sustain their children. You shouldn't disrespect your parents because they are old, if you are alive, you will get old too. You should give your parents their flowers while they are living.

It's important we should love our mothers; we should never forget how they suffered to bring us into this world. Not only do mothers protect but they give guidance to their children. My mother had died, and I miss her wisdom, love, and compassion. There were times when her tender voice gave hope to my disappointments. She would sit and tell me I will make it if I put God first. Don't look back at what you didn't do in the past, now is the time before another chance passed. Tell her how much you love her.

My jailhouse ministry was a time for me to share with the inmates the importance of loving their mothers. I do say, "If only you heed what your mothers and fathers taught you, you would be a better son or daughter."No one really knows about life until one had lived to a certain age. Yet, when God comes into our lives, He brings about a change in our lives.

Everybody has a right to enjoy life. We can choose the kind of job we want, but we have to learn how to be patient; we also need to be honest and fair. If we live the best we can, we will be able to help others live right. It took me forty years to get to a place in life where I became a blessing to others. Before my conversion, I was a bum and drunk, and I couldn't help my family. A man must provide for his loved ones, but wasn't the case with me. I would take my money and drink it up. Sadly, my family suffered due to my actions. I failed God; my family, wife, and children suffered because of my actions. God had given me a family to teach them the dangers of addictions and wayward women, and I failed them – I robbed them of hope. This might be one of the reasons why some people commit suicide; when they give up on hope.

After all of the name calling and evil things that I experienced, God gave me another chance. He has given me people to put my experiences in writing so that others who read it may be blessed.

I Am Only a Pluck Away

While walking alone in a field of beauty,
a voice came to me.

A familiar path it was to me
but never have I heard a pleading voice.

As the sun gave forth its radiant light,
a voice said to me,
"Why not pluck me today"?

"Pluck", I said! "Yes",
"Pluck me tenderly".

Today my gift is to be your gift,
not to keep but to give.

Dew has fallen upon my leaves,
and refreshing rains have strengthened me.

Now is time for me to share
what has been shared with me.

For within my buds are fragrance smiles.

Share my fragrance and bring a smile.

Do it now and see a smile.

And if, on the morrow,
you wish to give a smile;
I am only a pluck away.

By: Calvin C. Barlow, Jr.

Chapter 4

Faith

In 1983, I was fifty-one years of age, and that was the year I started walking by faith. Since that time, I have endured many things to stay faithful to my journey of faith. I have washed my clothes in a bucket to be decent for broadcast preaching. Many times, I went without the bare necessity to have enough funds for the radio ministry. For a period of twelve years, I went to jailhouse and nursing homes to minister. I never gave up because I believed my words would encourage someone about faith.

No one knows the future; I became a believer of God's word because God knows everything. I have learned that you need to have confidence in what you do. You don't give up when you don't see what you hope for, because faith is not seen. You have to have confidence in yourself and God to bring what you believe to pass; this has been my experience as I walked by faith. A faith journey can be complicated if you don't have faith in what you are doing. It has taken me thirty plus years to get this manuscript which talks about my life and all I have been through in writing. Disobedience to parents will cause one to suffer, the things I have suffered were caused by my disobedience, and this is the reason I am trying to warn people to change before they end up like me. Yet, I have confidence that what I have been through and what I share can help someone else.

You have to shun some things to keep you from causing heartaches and disappointments in people's lives. I know the consequences of not ignoring things that can cause harm to you and your family. I was a drunkard and it cost me my family. Alcoholics put more time in drinking and sampling the latest brew than taking care of their families. Alcohol takes over the mind and causes a person to act irresponsibly. In other words, you lose control of your mind. Alcohol allows people to dehumanize you, sometimes during my drunken episodes; people treated me like an animal because I permitted it with a smile on my face. Alcohol is deceptive, as it makes a person feel good while destroying the bodies. You may think you are having a good time, but in the near future it will cause suffering and you will have no other choice than to accept the mistakes of the past.

By faith, I took a shovel, hoe, and garden pick to work my land. During the last twenty years, I have worked an average of four acres per year, it is not that I regret the hard work, but if I had been educated, the work might have been easier. This is the reason I want to tell younger people to obey their parents and teachers. Life has a cost, but it's a price you don't have to pay if you learn how to be obedient. It is important that each generation share their wisdom with the next generation.

I have to enjoy life at an old age because I missed out on my opportunity while I was young. If you don't do right when you have the opportunity, life can be miserable. In other words, you will receive payment for your work: good or bad. It is best to admit you don't know everything. Prudent instructions can save you from later regrets and disappointments. I don't want people to end up like me; I cannot buy groceries without asking for help. If I go into a restaurant and the food is wrapped, I have to ask someone which is the hamburger or chicken sandwich. I cannot go to the restroom without asking which is for men or women. So if I were you, I would try my best to learn to read so I would not be ashamed to go anywhere.

Faith has to be put into action. Faith is no good to anyone who is not willing to apply it to life. Faith is powerless until it's put into action. Faith gave me something to help someone else. I found out faith is imperative when you are helping yourself and others. Faith will provide resources for the future. In fact, faith teaches us that life has stepping stones that help us to get to heaven. God rewards our trials and burdens with peace and contentment. Sometimes in life, we don't know where our blessings come from because our minds are so burdened with difficulties we forget our blessings. There were times in my life when the feeding of my hogs and pushing a wheelbarrow was a burden, but God has turned these burdens to blessings.

I was walking downtown one day when a man came up to me and asked me, "Do you want to buy a car?" I said yes! I want a car, but I cannot afford one. He said, "I have one to give you. In the month of May, 1996, I received the car. I had prayed that the Lord would bless me with one, and he brought it to pass. This is why it pays to be kind and good to everyone. That was when I started to experience miracles, and I told people how God was working miracles.

A fellow came to me from Aliceville and gave me a truck. At the time, I was working in Aliceville at the lumber mill. I was so fond of singing songs that my boss would get mad and curse me. I told him if I could not be happy while I worked on his job, he could have his job. So I walked off the job.

In a vision, God took me to the top of a mountain. I was going through some difficulty at the time. I did not understand what was going on. I told someone my vision, and he laughed, he thought I was losing my mind. When you are living by faith, it gives you hope to receive things that you don't understand.

I was standing with a shovel when I had a vision. I thought at that time it was my imagination. God was showing me the way and how to use what I had to make a living for myself. Ben Simpson took some pictures of me standing with my shovel in my hand. He also made the first video pictures of me with a shovel and a hoe. That's the way I farmed for some years. Often, people were surprised when I showed them the pictures. The pictures were made so my grandchildren and others could see how hard I worked to earn a living for myself. Life is about doing your best; yes, it was hard work for me.

I can't read or write, but I want my grandchildren to be educated and obedient to God's word. My faith has brought me a long way. There were times when I wanted to help them, and I couldn't assist because I didn't have the education that I needed to help them. I regret I couldn't be the father or grandfather I should have been. I couldn't do the things I was supposed to do, as I didn't have the knowledge it requires. Unfortunately, people can't undo the things they didn't do, we are forced to live with things we wish we had done.

You need faith. Every individual needs to have faith because life is filled with uncertainties. Faith will help you to do things right; things that would drive the average person crazy don't bother people of faith. Even when our actions are not pleasing to God or man, belief gives comfort. This is confusing, but belief is powerful. Often, people worry themselves about things they can't do anything about. Thus, faith allows you to cope with challenges.

I have learned through the years how to deal with things that come against me. When I was a child, I was odd from everybody else. One day, one of my teachers asked me a question, "How do you make friends with someone?" I responded to the question, "You have to be friendly in order to make friends." He thought I was one of the stupid ones. Today, it is the same way; in order to have friends you must be friendly yourself. This is how to develop a friendship.

It took me forty years to put my answer to the teacher's question into action. Understanding life's challenges are essential to living a healthy life. However, I wouldn't want anyone to take forty years to learn about life as I did. I consoled myself believing that since I am now a minister, God was teaching me a lesson to help others.

Older people have the knowledge to share with the younger generation because they have experienced many of life's challenges. If younger people listened to the olders, they could avoid some of the destructive consequences of life. My life has been filled with bad choices, and I can tell people that disobedience leads to disappointments.

In 1992, when I didn't have a truck, I use to gather my crops with a wheelbarrow. I would push the wheelbarrow with vegetables in it for miles. It is important to walk by faith. The Lord had shown me how people would treat me. I had seen how I would be mistreated by people in the churches. I am a living witness that your church members will abuse you. I have lived the things God told me. I knew if I walked upright, I would be looked over, talked about and misused. God showed me my household would be my worst enemy. Now, I have seen all these things come to pass.

Faith is nothing you can see. Faith is something you act upon because of your relationship with Christ. Faith without work is dead. The book of James declares that a man's faith and work are not separable. What man believes stands to be questioned. I recommend *The Book of Proverbs* which is the book of instructions for wisdom. This book was/is a revelation to people who are searching for answers to their problems. Taking the time to read *The Book of Proverbs* can help you with many of life's challenges. If you are having problems with your children, spouse, or business, you can find the answer in The Book of Proverbs.

Statement of Faith

I couldn't afford eyedrops or glasses, so I used Vaseline for years. I am using borrowed glasses now. My mother died and left me her glasses. It just came to me to use salt and sugar in my eyes. Now I can see well. If you live by faith, God will show you the way to use what you have. The Lord told me eleven years ago to step out in faith. Now, I can see the results of that. It did not make sense then, but now I see the sense it makes. God speaks to every individual, but you must take it by faith and not by sight.

John Earl Harris

Hold On

Hold on to hope, hold on to faith
When you come to the end of the rail
God's love is on the boundary
He will never let you fail
Believe in powers beyond you
When the way is dark without a light
There is never a place where God is not
Even in the caverns of the night
Hold on to hope, hold on to faith
God has a place that's just for you
Remember that God promises
His love will bring you through.

Chapter 5

Trust, Understanding, and Obedience

It's hard to trust people when you don't have confidence in yourself. When people lose trust in one another, it makes it hard to trust others. Everyone needs someone to trust. This is why I am trying to help people who find it hard to trust others. Children can benefit from knowing and learning from a person who has lived without proper education. Yet, is important have an education because it is hard to get a decent job. Technology has taken over, and it is the reason everyone needs to know how to read, write, and count. People can take advantage of you if you don't know how to read or write. When you cannot read or write, it requires that you always have someone by your side you can trust. I found out there is someone you can always trust; this can be your mother, father or anyone. There is always someone that is concerned about you getting an education. It is important for you to obey your teachers. Your teachers are concerned about you getting an education, although there are some that may not be so concerned. You need to take heed when they try to teach you, it's for your own benefit.

I really didn't realize how important education was until I had children. I didn't have enough knowledge to spell or write their names. Neither could I help them with their school work. I could not make a decent living as an adult because I did not have a proper education. This is why it is important to know that teachers are not against you; education gives you the tool to know people's motives. However, it is the responsibility of all parents to teach their children about trust and who they can trust.

These days, people don't want to discipline their children. The lack of parental control is wreaking havoc on our nation. Too many parents want other peoples' children to be punished for making bad choices while neglecting to correct their children. This is a mystery to me. Why do people think children will do right when they are not disciplined for wrong behavior? It is not fair when a child is raised without discipline. The Bible teaches parents to train their children; if we fail to obey The Bible, we are practicing a lifestyle against God, and we all will stand before God.

Everyone wants to be treated fairly; it is important to teach your children the difference between right and wrong. Destruction is coming upon parents because they are responsible for raising and teaching their children. Parents should teach their children how to love others when they are young. When children are taught correctly, they will not destroy, rob, or kill because they will have love for other people. Hatred makes men kill one another. Hatred has killed many people, but love will help you enjoy life.

God will judge everyone. Sometimes, a man and woman will break the law by trying to keep their children, husband, or wife from being punished for breaking a law. Everyone breaks the law sometimes; however, it is the same punishment for the poor and the rich. We all are supposed to get equal justice for any wrong doings.

Parents sometimes think teachers and principal are misusing their children. This is due to the fact that most parents don't take time to find out what is going on. Too many parents are indulging in personal pleasures and are not concerned with their children's education and welfare. Many parents give more time to their jobs than they spend with their children, yet, the bible teaches that children are the heritage of God. We need to spend time with our kids. We need to take enough time to show them we love them. Parents need to show children how to live. Love plays a role in everything we do, even cats and dogs want some love.

Chapter 6

Love

Love is a four letter word; it is powerful than an atomic bomb. It is something each and every individual deserves because it is more valuable than silver or gold. It's something man or woman cannot buy. It's the most precious thing in the world. It is can be expressed. No one has ever fully understood where love came from, but it has been handed down from generation to generation. Everyone wants to be loved; the average person doesn't love someone that doesn't love them back. God's love outlasts all other types of love. He makes you understand not to give up if someone does not like you; this makes you strive for better understanding. A man and a woman will have a better outlook in life if they could keep their mind and heart together. This is why I want you to understand that life is depending on you. We all love somebody. If you have love, you can follow and exhibit it through life without giving up.

Love is something no man can explain; it has never been explained by man, woman, or child. It is something that is so deep that even science has not been able to explain it. Love can't be bought; sometimes you don't know the reason you love who you love. Some people fall in love with persons that don't love them. Love is something you can't make. Love is a word that everyone says, but they don't understand what it really is.

So many people get carried away in the name of love. This is why you should examine it yourself. So many people have lost their wife or husband for lack of love; homes have been broken up due to the absence of the words "I love you." Many lives have been taken by taking the word "love" in vain. Everyone feels good when they hear words of love; it's a sweet word and everyone loves to hear sweet words about themselves. This is why people are fond of saying "I love you", even when they don't mean it; we should take the time to carefully analyze these sweet words. It makes you comfortable when people are saying good things about you but you need to be careful. Real love will bring joy, peace, and happiness. Be careful not to be caught up in sweet words, it can cause you unhappiness.

Love carries a lot of power, and it will help you to understand others. People don't know the value of love, if people knew how powerful love is, they would understand one another. Love is powerful, if each individual knew about love, it would make us understand one another, but because we don't understand love, we don't value it. Love will make a woman and man understand one another. People would love their wife, husband, mother, father, and children if they understood what love was. Money doesn't make love; some people even think that sex makes love; love will come on its own. You cannot make love with an evil mind or heart. You need to understand what love is about.

I have tried some of these things. I have experience in what I am getting someone to write about. Love will not let you hurt someone you love. If you loved them and then hurt them, then you don't have the love of God on the inside; you cannot hurt the people you love. I have learned through the years that love is a powerful weapon indeed.

Love is something you can't fully express, explain, or resist; you don't know why because it is a mystery to mankind, we have never been able to show or tell it enough. Everyone that loves has something in common; love is a good thing to have. If you find someone that loves you, it makes life extraordinary, and it gives you something to look forward to; yet, the experience can be miserable if you love someone that doesn't love you in return. God's love is not puffed up because he is concerned about everyone; God loves in spite of all we do or say. This is why we should keep the love of God in our hearts. No matter what we think or do, it doesn't keep God from loving each and every one of us. Man's love is not greater than the love of God; I'd rather be loved by God than any man. Mankind has never been able to express love in its purest form; we have never been able to explain it either; it is beyond man's knowledge. This is my understanding of love, and I hope you understand more about it and do better in life.

LOVE

Love is a blessing so hard to explain

It flows from your heart like the pouring of rain

Such a gift from our heart that lights up each day

To be capable of it is what we say

There are so many loves that a person can render

The love for our wife is so tender

So much love that we have for our daughters and sons

For our parents and friends and for everyone

But the love that surpasses all the others we know

Should be from our heart that would continually grow

By: Tammy Jones

Be Happy Recipe

When your day is dreary

and you're feeling sad,

think of something cheerful

to lift and make you glad.

If you're having problems,

you are not alone.

Life's no a bed of roses,

everyone has some.

If sorrow overtakes you,

he comforts with his love,

Count your many blessings,

help someone in need.

Doubt and fear will lessen,

and joy is yours indeed.

Chapter 7

The Importance of Attitude

As I said before, the vision started around 1983. When I began to tell people all about it, they thought I was crazy. I wanted to prevent people from destruction. I wanted to tell them I wasted so many years of my life by being disobedient. I didn't understand what was going on, but my attitude was doing the damage all those years. People tried and took their time to help me. I couldn't be helped because of my attitude. Attitude is defined as a way of acting, feeling, thinking, or a mental position. Your attitude will cause people not to help you if you have a nasty one. If you have a good attitude, people will be glad to help you. This is why I am trying to let you know how much damage I did to myself because of my attitude.

You have to watch your attitude because it can do much damage if care is not taken. People can't help you because you won't listen to them or follow instructions. Your attitude will make you feel like you don't need help from others, and it will destroy you. This goes for all individuals that won't take instructions. The people that are trying to help you can be a mother, father, teacher, doctor, lawyer, or whoever wishes you good.

This is why each individual needs to help someone. When our attitude isn't right with man and God, it will destroy us. We have to pray to God for help because we cannot do it on our own. Satan will make you think you are right, but you have to pray and keep your faith in God. He will help you keep the right attitude.

Chapter 8

The Importance of People

Oftentimes, men and women do not value themselves and others. If they did, they wouldn't destroy themselves and others. Perhaps, they are destructive because they don't feel important and needed. As a child, I often wondered why grown folks whipped other people's children. I had a dream where my mother flogged a child. In a situation like this, the parent of the child need to understand that the other parent is not intentionally abusing the child. This is a practice that has been passed onto future generations in some black communities where elders can discipline other people's children.

I started to walk by faith in 1983, but before then, I lived a wasteful and undisciplined life. I abused my body and mind. It's important for people to take care of their bodies so they can enjoy life. The fact is --"you will reap what you sow." Alcohol and dope will damage your body. It is critical for people to know the things that will harm their bodies.

We have to live with the consequences of our decisions, and it's hard to live with someone you don't understand. It is important to take care of yourselves, so you can live longer and happy. A person that is sick all the time cannot enjoy life. Thus, I wouldn't have had to suffer the ills of life if I had taken heed to corrections of people who had already experienced life. This is why it is important to share this information so that others might not miss their opportunities in life. Choices have consequences and can affect future job opportunities. I have been down that road, and I speak from the revelation of God.

There are three groups critical to a family: husbands, wives, and children. The well-being of the family unit determines the health of society.

Husband and Wife

Husband and wife cannot enjoy each other when they cannot communicate. Living together and not having anything in common will lead to a broken relationship. When couples make mistakes in their relationship, it can only be healed when they become honest with each other. When one admits to a wrong, it allows the healing process to begin. The relationship of a couple is an agreement sealed by trust, and when the trust is violated, love and truthfulness are the only remedies that can heal it.

Anyone who has a husband or wife should show him/her love. Couples need to appreciate what their partner does and encourage one another because that is part of life. I have learned that because my wife and I have separated. It is important to support your spouse, care for them as well as love them. My sharing about commitment between a man and his wife is not based on the writing of books, but a life lived with regrets and observation.

Children

The lives of children are being destroyed when mothers and fathers fail to discipline them for wrong doings. They will get to a point where they think that what they are doing is right. This is what happens when you don't discipline them. They are going to talk back at you, and then you wonder why your children act the way they do. The Bible says if you don't discipline the child, you will ruin him/her. This is why children are doing what they are doing in school. We need to let parents know how they can help their children by teaching them in love. If they are taught to love one another, they will have better relationship with their parents. If the mother and father don't teach the children what they are supposed to do, they will be a problem in the future. When the child doesn't have to work, he/she thinks that is right. However, if they are taught how to love, love will keep them from destroying one another.

You shouldn't get mad at your mother or father because they make decisions for you. I don't want you to make the same mistakes I made. It took me sixty-four years to tell my story. The choices you make today, you have to live with. Sometimes, it can bring hatred towards your mother and father. When your child is young, you should teach him/her about heartaches, disappointments, and if they don't have branded clothes or shoes to wear like other children, you need to show and tell them how to face life.

Communication

Lack of effective communication will make people destroy one another. People don't know how to communicate with one another. Even computers have to communicate with each other; when computers don't communicate, there are a lot of problems. Airplanes and trains crash when there is no proper communication with the control center. Lack of proper communication can destroy a lot of innocent people. This is why everyone needs to play his or her part. We can be of great help to one another.

I was never able to communicate because people thought I was boasting or bragging about what was going to happen. Now, I understand how important it is to be able to communicate with others. This is why people find it difficult to talk to each other. Jealousy can cause people to misunderstand others. Everyone is not alike and doesn't think alike. Love will help people communicate with one another. Everyone needs someone they can communicate with without having the pressure of being seen as crazy, feeling inferior or superior to another person. If you love, you can talk to anybody.

No one knows the heart and mind of the other person. We make mistakes trying to determine the motives of others. We all make mistakes. This is why everyone should seek to understand the other man.

I have been through it, and I am still going through some difficult times. After all that I have been through, I cry sometimes. The sharing of my life's journey is a blessing to me. God has allowed me to live a life of repentance and blessings. I have learned that a sacrifice comes with a future benefit. I tell people who don't have a job to use the time to prepare for their future. I can testify that when we fail to use the down time as preparation time, we will miss out on future opportunities. I didn't plan for the future, and I suffered the consequences. Whatever you do, don't blame others for your sufferings. Sometimes, suffering is the consequence of failing to act responsibly. Get an education, so you will be qualified for the job. Don't get mad at others because they took advantage of the opportunity that you wasted.

A lot of people don't want to take responsibility. When people fail to take responsibility for their actions, it causes conflict. We all have a role to play in life if justice is to be for all. We have been created to help each other and to treat others as we wish to be treated. The failure to adhere to this fundamental principle is the reason for killing, confusion, stealing, and rape in our communities. We are supposed to be concerned about others. We are supposed to help one another overcome mistakes. We should be able to take responsibilities for the benefit of our children, grandchildren, and future generations.

It is important to teach children to listen to their parents. We should teach our kids that living a life according to God's word can prevent them from life's problems. Also, listening to others can help one avoid the mistakes others have made by being hardheaded. Yes, I have suffered tremendously because of being hardheaded. The question is, "Why would you want to suffer because of disobedience?"

I have come to this conclusion that I have missed out. I wasted my time, and now I see what I should have done. Since I cannot do those things that I should have done, I can help others. You have time to get your education. It came to my mind to speak so that you may know it is not from me but from God. This is the end of the revelation that came to me to let everyone know how important people are to God and themselves. I am a living witness to the fact that you can't get a proper job without an education. I came to this conclusion also: if you don't start on time, you will be miserable trying to make a living.

Letter from a Friend

I just had to write to tell you how much I love you and care for you.

Yesterday, I saw you walking and laughing with your friends, I hope that soon you'd want me to walk along with you too. So I painted you a sunset to close your day and whispered a cool breeze to refresh you. I waited… you never called…I just kept on loving you.

As I watched you fall asleep last night, I wanted so much to touch you. I spilled moonlight onto your face…trickling down your cheeks as so many tears have. You didn't even think of me; I wanted so much to comfort you.

The next day I exploded a brilliant sunrise into glorious morning for you. But you woke up late and rushed off to work…you didn't even notice. My sky became cloudy, and my tears were the rain.

I love you. Oh, if you'd only listen. I really love you. I try to say it in the quiet of the green meadow and in the blue sky. The wind whispers my love throughout the treetop and spills it into the vibrant colors of all the flowers. I shouted it to you in the thunder of the great waterfalls and composed love songs for birds to sing for you. I warmed you with the clothing of my sunshine and perfumed the air with nature's sweet scent. My love for you is deeper than any ocean, and greater than any need in your heart. If you'd only realize how much I care.

My dad sends his love. I want you to meet him…he cares too. Fathers are just that way. So please call on me soon. No matter how long it takes, I'll wait…because I love you.

Your Friend,

Jesus

Chapter 9

The Importance of Education

We don't put enough emphasis on education. Children don't strive to receive an education because they don't know the value of it. After they are grown, they will find out when they try to find a job that they don't have enough education to qualify for the job. The average child will begrudge the person who told him he is not qualified for a job. This is where the confusion starts. Mothers and fathers need to work together to teach their children. They need to work with teachers. Parents accuse teachers for their children's failure to achieve in the classroom when they don't know who is causing the conflict. This makes the teacher's job hard.

Some parents don't know how to help their children with their school work. When you don't know how to help your child, you need to ask someone who knows how to go about it. Education is paramount because computers are taking over, and the child will need to have the education to get a good paying job. We need to put all the efforts we can into educating our children. We need to do all we know how to do to help our children receive the education they really need. They are important to us. This is why every mother and father needs to put all their effort into their children's education. If they get a good education, they can get a good paying job.

Education

Education is paramount to everyone. It is important because it teaches one how to read, speak correctly, and comprehend. In today's society, education plays an important role. You need education to get a decent job, learn to cook, drive a car, read signs and map, and just about how to do anything. If you lose out on your education, you have lost out on everything. Stay in school and learn all that you can because you will need it. Be a winner ☺ not a quitter☹!

By: Christina Harris

Chapter 10

Expressions of Thanksgivings

    I, Clarence Tate give honor to the Almighty God, who is the head of my life right now. I am also thankful for each day He blesses me with. First, I thank God for every eye that reads this, and for Brother Harris who is a great inspiration; anybody that's on fire like him for the Lord, can't help but inspire you (smiles). Well, I started out wrong at an early age, around thirteen years old to be precise; I joined a church that I soon fell away from. My parents often send me to church, but somehow I would end up somewhere else. Don't get me wrong, I have always believed that God did exist. I just didn't know how to accept who He really is. That's when I broke God's commandment – "honor thy father and mother," and so I broke another one until I was 29 years old. That was a long time for me to keep being disobedient toward God and man. I broke this commandment that I am paying half of my freedom by being confined to prison. I thank God for sparing me to be alive, to have a chance; for his mercy and for his forgiveness. Thank you,

Lord! I could go on and on but I am closing now. My prayers are with you all. May God bless and strengthen you in faith. Please don't give up on God!

By: Clarence Tate

My Testimony

My testimony for the lord Jesus Christ happened on a Wednesday night during the month of November, 1994. I received Jesus Christ back into my life as my Lord and Savior. I had backslided, but God is married to backsliders. A messenger of God came to me. However, I was ready to repent and turn from the wrong doings I was involved in.

Being a victim of crack cocaine, I was headed for destruction. After being arrested for committing a crime to obtain money to buy crack, I knew then that I was at the end of my rope. I tried all kinds of ways to find peace of mind within myself. All of those things failed. I had one more option, and that was to try Jesus again. Being brought up in a Christian environment, I have a real zeal for God. I, however, wasn't living a life based on the Christianity that I had been taught.

That Wednesday night, I asked Jesus to come into my life, and I surrendered all to him. As I was confessing my sins, I began to cry. Tears ran down my face as I knelt on the floor of the jail cell. A particular burning sensation came over my body. I closed my eyes, and as I did, calmness came over my body and a voice said to me, "Anthony, your sins are forgiven." The man was dressed in a long gown and was standing about ten feet in front of me. His hands were outstretched towards me, beckoning unto me to come. At that moment, I opened my eyes, and he was gone. Others that were in and out of the cell asked, "What happened?" I told them to the best of my ability. Since that night, my attitude toward life changed completely. The Holy Spirit has been and continues to lead me from day to day. Every day is a blessing to be able to tell someone about Jesus Christ, his love and the mercy he has shown me. I thank God for his "grace and mercy", for giving me another chance to get myself right with him.

Presently, I'm still in Pickens County Jail. I am continuing to be a witness for Jesus Christ. I've seen a lot of miracles performed while in here. Prisoners have come and gone. Some are prior inmates because they failed to walk with Christ while they walked out the front door. Every day we must live for God as though that is our last here on earth. If you haven't tried Jesus today, don't you think it's about time you do? "Glory be to the King of Kings."

By: Anthony Gray

Christmas 1994

May the true spirit of Christmas bring you peace and happiness!

Brother Harris-We are so thankful that God who sent you to this jail. Your work is not in vain. May God bless you, our prayers are with you.

Men of the Pickens County Jail
Ronnie McGill
Clarence Tate
Garrett Gaines
Tim Hollinger
Jeffery Lindsey
Raymond Mayhew
Anthony Gary

Education

I wish I could read what I see.

I wish I could write what my mind says to me.

My eyes see what my mind doesn't understand.

My mind speaks words that my hands cannot repeat.

Oh! Just for a moment, what a joy it would be

If my hands could repeat what my mind says to me.

Then my hands could tell the story of my eyes,

And if you are like me, education is best for you.

A guide for the hands and a tutor for the eyes

That's what education is to me.

By: Calvin C. Barlow, Jr.

Chapter 11

Expressions of Thanksgivings

Everybody is trying to find answers to issues in their lives. Sometimes it takes people longer to find the answers they need. The answer is in the word of God. It is a mystery. Those that take heed to the word of God know that the answer is being obedient to the word of God. Many people have testified to finding answers to the situations of their lives by being obedient to the word of God. It took me forty years to find the response to what God had for man and woman. This is why I don't want anyone to miss their blessings by being disobedient to God; being defiant leads to destruction. I have come to a conclusion out of all my findings, that you need to be obedient to man and God. The enjoyment of life is based on being obedient to God and having respect for mankind. This is a revelation that God showed me to share with others. All nations have to stand for themselves. Don't miss your opportunity: obey and trust God. I am a living witness that heavenly faith can be used to accomplish earthly goals. Remember, the spiritual man will understand spiritual things and natural man will understand natural things.

Quotations and Anecdotes/Scripture

How to Conquer Fear

- And when I saw him, I fell at his feet as dead. And He laid his right hand on me saying fear not, I am the first and the last.

- This is a lesson that every person needs to learn. We need to know how to conquer fears. Fear is real. We all face it as we move through life. Fear is a deadly emotion that paralyzes man and makes him unproductive.

- Fear will cause you to lose sleep and lose good health. Fear will destroy you. This kind of fear does not come from the Lord. You ask me if fear does not come from the Lord, then where does it come from?

- Crippling and deadly fear come from the enemy and Satan. Let's hear what the Apostle Paul had to say in 2nd Timothy Chapter One and Verse Seven. He says, "For God has given us the spirit of love and a spirit of sound mind." What God has given us is called self-control and self-discipline.

- Remember that we are discussing something greater than being concerned. I know from time to time, we all become concerned about different matters, but we must not let them overtake us and cause us to become unproductive.

- According to the modern scientists, there are seventy-nine distinct categories of fear. There are some people who are afraid of everything. There are some people who are afraid of cats, rats, chickens, and cows… you name it.

- There are some people that are afraid of other people. They are afraid of heights, underground tunnels, and pain. Some people are even afraid of being alone, being married, and dead bodies. There are people who hate the past, dislike the present and are afraid of the future.

- There are some people who are afraid of their own shadows. There is a story of a man who was going to a graveyard and fell into a freshly dug grave. The grave was about six feet deep, and he tried hard to get out. He began jumping and screaming to get out. Finally, he gave up and said to himself I can't get out of here. I will just sit down and be quiet until someone comes along and get me out of here. Finally, another man came along into the graveyard, and he slipped and fell into the same grave. He jumped and tried to get out, but he also could not get out. Then he heard a voice saying, "You can't get out of here, just sit and be quiet."

- There is another story about fear. One day a stranger stopped by a house looking for some food. The man of the house invited him in and told him they were just about to eat dinner. The stranger took a seat at the table. The man of the house said, "I will go down to the cellar to get a bottle of wine." He stayed in the cellar so long that his wife went to see what was wrong. She found him sitting on the stairs crying. She asked him why he was crying. He told her to look-up. An ax was stuck in the ceiling of the cellar. He said, "One day it will fall and kill one of us." She took a seat beside him and began to cry. The daughter decided to go to the cellar to see what was wrong. When she saw her parents crying, she asked what was wrong. They told her about the ax stuck in the ceiling of the cellar. She sat down beside her parents and began to cry. They took so long in the cellar that the stranger decided to check on them. He found them sitting on the stairs of the cellar crying. He asked what was wrong. They showed him the ax and told him that one day someone would come down to get a bottle of wine, and the ax will fall on that person. With a smile on his face, the stranger took the ax out of the ceiling and said, "Calm your fears. I know a man that will come in the hour of fear." He will say, "Fear not for I have come to save you."

When the disciples were in the midst of the storm, he came to them saying fear not it is I, then he spoke to the storm. I can join in with the hymn writer who says what have I to dread, what have I to fear… leaning on the Everlasting arm. I have perfect peace with my Lord so dear, leaning on the everlasting arm.

- ❖ Fear comes when you lose control. A principal cause of fear is found in the book of Genesis. God created Adam and Eve and gave them the power over the earth. But, when sin entered fear also came in. It caused Adam and Eve to run and hide from God.

- ❖ Fear makes us believe that judgment is coming. That is why we run. Have you ever driven through a red light, and then you drive a mile or two looking back with fear? That is because you knew you were wrong, and you are expecting judgment.

- ❖ Fear comes when you sense that you have lost control. You fear your children if you sense you have lost control over them. You will fear your husband or wife if you think you have lost control. Unfortunately, people are accustomed to managing other people but God never told any man to control the other person, but to love one another. We are to control things, but we are not to control people. We are to love people.

Sometimes, even in the church, there are those who try to control other people's destiny. Don't let others control you. Tell them you are created in the image of God and you must follow Him. We must follow the Captain H.I.M. not the little him. Where he leads me, I will follow. I will go with him all the way. For the Lord is my shepherd. I shall not want. He maketh me to lie down in green pastures. He leadeth me beside still waters. He restoreth my soul. He leadeth me in the paths of righteousness for his name sake. Yea, though I walk through the valley of the shadow of death. I will fear no evil, for thou art with me. Thy rod and thy staff, they comfort me. Thou preparest a table before me in the presence of my enemies. Thou anointest my head with oil. My cup runneth over. Surely, goodness and mercy shall follow me all the days of my life, and I will dwell in the house of the Lord forever and ever.

❖ The Lord is my light and my salvation. Who shall I fear? The Lord is the strength of my life, of whom shall I be afraid? Have no fear. Fret not thyself because of evil doers; neither be thou envious of the worker of iniquity for they shall soon be cut down like grass and wither like the green herb.

❖ Trust in the Lord and do good so shalt thou dwell in the land, and verily thou shall be fed. Fear will make you say wrong things at the wrong time. There was a man who had a horse, and he sold it to another man. He had trained the horse to move at his command. When he said thank you, the horse would start walking. When he said thank you, Lord, the horse would start trotting. Whenever he said thank you, thank you, Lord, the horse would run as fast as it could. When he said amen, the horse would stop. The man bought the horse and decided to ride it home.

The man said thank you, and the horse began to walk. The man said thank you Lord and the horse began to trot. The man said thank you, thank you Lord and the horse began to run as fast as it could. The man looked up and saw a cliff in front of him and out of fear he forgot the command to make the horse stop. He cried, "O my Lord, what do I say to stop this horse? He remembered and said amen. Yet, while wiping the sweat from his brows, he said, "Thank you Lord" and over the cliff he went with the horse.

- ❖ John Chapter Four and Verse Eighteen says that there is no fear at all in God's love. Perfect love casts out fear. God's love and fear cannot remain in the same house. They can't live together.

- ❖ Think about it, if you have not totally surrendered yourself to Jesus Christ, you are still trying to protect yourself. And the devil is telling you to use your five senses. If we are not in Christ, we don't like the covers being pulled off us. We work really hard at trying to keep the covers up.

  Have no fear; just be honest enough to say, Lord, it is me. Yes, I am willing to obey you. That is how we grow beyond fear. This is how we overcome and defeat fear and the devil. To conquer fear demands that we become honest with God.

- ❖ The devil can have you thinking that you are standing right with God. But the Holy Spirit will show you where you really are. Oh, if you would listen to him, he will show you where you stand with Him.

- ❖ You may think that you have victory in your life, and the anointing of God is indeed operating and working through you. Actually, you may be setting yourself up for a fall. Let me ask you a question. Have you given all of yourself to the Lord? Is it all on the altar of sacrifice? Does the Spirit control your body and soul? You can only be blessed as you yield your body and soul to the Lord. Can you see dark crevices in your own heart? You may think that you are in control of yourself and that you are secure. This is why so many people cannot put their all on the altar for God. They fear that there will be nothing in return for them. I heard David say, "I have never seen the righteous forsaken or their seed begging bread." You won't experience blessings until you become honest with God. Oh, it is easy to go to church and sit in the pew and say amen. But we must hear what the Spirit is saying to us, then do it, and say Amen. Here comes a question: have you given your all to God? I am talking about the real you; that which cannot be seen with the eye of man. The real you that God sees and knows; fear keeps you from giving God your best. But when you fall in love with the perfect love, when you come to trust the perfect love; you will stop believing in your own security.

- ❖ One way to defeat fear is to pray. Pray often, pray sincerely, prayer is more than coming into the Sanctuary or kneeling at the altar. Whenever you pray, cry out to God…out of your spirit with a sincere heart. If you are angry, tell him. Be honest with God. Continue to empty yourself and all of your frustrations and the Holy Ghost will take over, and you tell God how much you love him. You must empty yourself. If you are living in fear, you must admit it. If you are afraid, ask God to help you. Let the word of God dwell in your heart. Let the Word become your dwelling place.

- ❖ To conquer your fears, you must enter into a confession of faith and declare freedom from fear. Faith comes by hearing and hearing by the word of God. We must tell the devil that God has not given us a spirit of fear.

- ❖ There are three kinds of fears that you must conquer before you can enjoy life. The first fear is the fear of life. Some people fear living. They wake up every day saying, "Oh. Is it morning?" What they should be saying is good morning Lord; I thank you for another day."

- Some folks have fear about their tomorrow. Do you know who holds tomorrow? Do you know who holds your future? Do you know who 'the first and the last' is? Do you know who is in charge of your past and present? God is in charge.

  He said, "I am the resurrection and the life. He that believes in me though dead, yet he shall live."

  Why do you think the rate of suicide is going up? People are afraid to live, so they kill themselves. People who are addicted to alcohol and drugs are people who are afraid to live.

- There are those who fear life's responsibilities. Will I be a success in my business? Am I going to disappoint my family? Will they accept me?

- Some Christians have fears; they believe they can't hold on to things, they say if you give it to me, I am going to mess it up. I always mess up things. Everything I touch goes sour. I am just a follower. Don't give me any responsibilities.

- If you are a born again believer in Jesus Christ, you have been given responsibilities. You are to do more than sitting in the pews absorbing the worship during services. You are to take your moment in worship and share it with someone else. Don't you know that Jesus is no longer on the cross? He is alive and very well. We have the responsibility to share the "Good News" with the world. We are commanded to tell other about the goodness of the Lord.

- There is the fear of death. Most people are afraid of death. But as we walk with Jesus, he will take away the fear of death. Being baptized in the Holy Spirit removes the fear of death, even though we walk through valleys of death, we know that God is with us. We become aware that the body can be destroyed, but only God can destroy the soul. We are made aware that we have another body not made by the hand of man, but one that's eternal.

- The Lord tells us to bear one another's burdens. But he never told us to be other people's crutch. We must pray continuously. Know that the prayer of the righteous avails much.

- Conquer your fears. Look to the hill from whence cometh your help. Look up and look up to God. Let us pray that God delivers us from the spirit of fear that we might defeat the devil. Ask him to take away the fear and to give you the spirit of love and of sound mind. God is able to drive away all fear. Look within and pray this prayer: Lord, please deliver me from my insecurities and fears. Amen.

The Beauty of Jesus

Let the beauty of Jesus, be seen in me
All His wonderful passion and purity!
O Thou Spirit divine, all my nature refine,
Til the beauty of Jesus be seen in me.

Take heed to what you see and hear,
For it affects your soul;
Be sure it's pleasing to the Lord
And that he's in control.

For answered prayer we thank you, Lord;
We know you're always there
To hear us when we call on you
We're grateful for your care.

http://davidroper.blogspot.com/2015_01_01_archive.html

Appendix 1

Newspaper Articles:

"John Earl Harris": This Man Practices Faith with a Shovel
By: Rev. James Purnell
Pastor of Stansel Baptist Church

John Earl Harris wears a coat of many colors. He was birthed and grew up in the Stansel Community and is known by his friends as "Papa Harris." He farms, sells, and gives away his produce. He also preaches and ministers to those who are "down and out" and need encouragement. John Earl has a simple but wise philosophy of life, "Take what you have, do the best you can with it, and use it to glorify God." This is what led him to truck farming.

The Stansel's native had worked most of his adult life doing "public work", most of which was at sawmills. About ten years ago, he decided that he wanted to farm but he did not have the equipment. All the tools he owned were a shovel and a hoe. He started with that and while breaking his garden spot and visualizing the kind of crops he wanted to grow, he says he heard a voice from above telling him to use what he had and that he would be blessed.

For about two years, the determined farmer worked about 15 acres with a shovel and a hoe. He depended on Mr. Ben and others to break his patches when they could, but much of his crops were tended by hand. He was already selling and furnishing the neighbors with turnips and collards and would have English peas coming in around the 1st of June. Papa also grows a lot of other vegetables. He had already planted sweet corn, watermelons, muskmelon, and planned to plant peas, bean, squash, and oak as soon as the weather permitted.

After that, Stansel Baptist Church said, "We are buying him a new motor for this tilter and hope to soon relieve him of some of his hoe and shovel work. We believe that he is a unique man who has done so much with such limited resources has a message that needs to be told. His testimony proves that God's resources are not limited.

With a determined will, strength, and a hoe and shovel, mountains can be moved even if it is all we have to work with. Just think of what could have done with that kind of faith combined with the massive technology we have today. If Jesus feeds more than 5,000 people with some fish and a few loaves of bread, Papa Harris believes God can take things like a shovel and a hoe and use them to feed and bless people.

Grows Large Turnips, Shares Message of Faith

John Earl "Minister" Harris, 66 of Reform, recently grew this 4½ pound turnip at his home. Harris said he has been working in his garden for 14 years with only a shovel and hoe, and depends on his faith in God to sustain him. He said his mission in life is to share one message to young people: success depends on a good education, along with faith in action, knowledge and understanding, love with power; he added that it is hard to get a good job without an education today.

John Earl Harris

In fact, he grows about every vegetable you can think of; corn, tomatoes, and watermelons are his favorites. If you think garden fresh vegetables you need to get to know this man. He has proven that you can take what you have, work hard with it and God will bless it. This is what he tells the people. He preaches to them in the jail. He says that young folks need to know this and he has been preaching and ministering at the Pickens County Jail now for thirteen years where he had weekly services. He says that he does not have to worry about those folks walking out on him. He also preached at the Nursing home in Reform for about twelve years. He says that he knows how hard life can be and considers his ministry one of faith and relies on God to help him support it. Papa Harris is 59 years old on this picture. He believes that faith in God and hard work is what keeps him going. His kind spirit and compassion for those who are struggling and hurting are known by the people of their areas, denominations, and races. A couple of ladies saw him in the Baptist Center one day and asked him if he was a preacher who had visited their church, he replied that he was and was willing to visit and share with any church who invites him. He said that he has some videos that show some of his hand-produced crops and is willing to loan them.

It has been said by different people that I would never get a book written about my life. I have proof of what I have said years ago. So when I was saying these things, I thought it was my imagination. All those years went by and it looked like it would never come true. Someone would start writing it but they would stop. I thought I would never get this book completed.

In my mind and heart, I knew what I wanted to complete it, but I thought it was impossible. I knew it could be done, but I could not do it myself. I thought I would have to give it up. Then, a lady came home to see after her mother and God laid it in her heart to help me. My dreams and visions have come true. This is reason I want to thank everyone that took the time to work with me. This is also why I can give this testimony. I had given up hope. I wrote two books. One is *Knowledge & Understanding*; the second book is *All about Faith*. This is the book people said that I would never get done. I could not do it and I had no one to do it for me. I have a witness that it is finished. I have the same faith that I had thirteen years ago. I have combined those two books into one and it is called *Two-Fold Books into One Book*.

I waited until I had someone that could help me and that seemed interested in what I was trying to do. You cannot find people to help you if you do not try to help yourself. I thank all those that made it possible for me and helped me. If it had not been for you, I would not have been able to help people that listen to me on the radio.

I started out on the radio twenty years ago. I have had many people come and say to me how they were enjoying it. Now I can see of what value faith is to those that have faith. Faith and love have greater power than anything on this earth. If man could only have love and faith in God and himself, he could see the blessing of faith.

Faith manifests itself by power. Anyone that has faith has power beyond measure. When love and faith mix they have greater power. Love seems to be what makes faith come into action. I did not know how powerful faith was until I took faith on. Down through the years as time passed, God got more powerful to me. I thought sometimes things were impossible, but I found out that all things are possible.

I bought two trailers then gave one out because I felt the need to help someone. The one left with me was faulty, but I thought that I would be able to fix it. I had to get someone to pull it for me. As they were pulling the trailer, they got it into a ditch. I had to have someone pull it out of the ditch.

In the end, they tore the trailer up and there was need for me to get another one. I believed that God was going to give me another one. However, I asked the Lord for a car instead and He gave me one. I had the car, although I had to get it fixed when I brought it. I had to take money to get it fixed.

He showed me another vision that he was going to give me a wife someday. Then, I looked forward to God manifesting the day and time. This is what I came to let the people know: if you walked by faith, God will manifest faith. Faith is not something that you can see. I stepped out in faith for 16 years and I still have some of the things that God showed me. Some of them had come to pass in 1998.

Rose of Sharon, a church in Hughes Town, is the same church I named *Hughes Temple*. There were preachers in Hughes Town. Their names are Bruce Hughes and Roy Hughes. I told them after I had finished what the Lord told me to do. The Lord wanted a church in Hughes Town and it had come to pass. Everything I have said has come to be true. I had a dream where the Lord took me to the top of a mountain, spoke to me, and I believe that he did this for me to help someone. I came to the conclusion that faith and love are the most powerful things here on earth.

Appendix 2

Messages Excerpts by John Earl Harris

What Is Destroying the People?

What is destroying the people is that they do not want to face up to their responsibilities. This is a mystery… And when you do not want to accept the things you get into or the things that you did when you were a child, it becomes so hard to accept life. Sometimes, humans do not want to be responsible for the things that they did or did not do to make life better for the future. So many people seem to destroy themselves because they shy away from responsibilities.

I say this because when I was a child I did not do certain things I ought to have done for my family. This is, perhaps, one of the reasons I thought it wise to share some of my experiences with the next generation of people. I am trying to help the next generation so they would not have to suffer for being hard headed - disobedient to their parents and disobedient to God. I learned at an old age that things that you should have done make a big difference when you have to face the people you consciously or unconsciously hurt by not doing the right things. This is the mystery of life. It is what makes it so hard to warn other people if they have never been through the same experience. It is just hard to express to others what will happen if they do not do certain things right. It pains me that it is so hard to explain to others about something they have never experienced. Some people have never suffered in order to make it better for others.

This is my knowledge of trying to tell the children about their mother and father; trying to express themselves so they do not bring so much sorrow or distress or pressure upon themselves. This is what I have experienced about life. There are certain things that a mother and father have experienced. They are the ones trying to get their children ready for facing disappointments. They have already experienced all that and they are trying to explain so that you do not have to get battered the way they did. What love could be more than that?

So, the Lord gave me the knowledge to pass this onto others. It would destroy the average human if they do to others what they cannot accept - because every man and woman, boy and girl will reap what they sow. Perhaps, what makes it so hard for them to understand is because they have never been in such positions. Some things are just too hard to believe sometimes. Notwithstanding, a boy and girl should have enough confidence in their parents that they would lead them right. Parents on their part have to follow the instructions of God's word.

After series of deep thoughts about these things, I came to the conclusion that mistreating others will not lead to good success. We all have to realize that each and every individual has feelings. It hurts when we do not consult them. So, this is why we ought to have enough respect for a mother and a father. Sincerely, it is going to come to a point in life when we are going to have to reap the same thing that we did to others. This reality is so hard for people to accept; it is complicated to know something they have not experienced. This message might sound too ordinary, yet it is what God gave me to pass on to others so they would not miss out on the opportunity to do better.

Being Hard-Headed Brings Much Sorrow

Being hard-headed could sometimes be enjoyable, especially when it gives one satisfaction to displease others. This singular reason is why I am trying to explain to each and every individual that would understand that being hard-headed causes many sorrows. I know because as a child, when my teacher would try to get me to learn, I would not attention because I thought was hurting her, but I was hurting myself. I did not know what the future was going to be like. Older people have the experience and that was why they were telling me about getting a good paying job so I could get recognized and be empowered with the power of expression. Then I would not be ashamed and would be able to withstand the pressure of life. The truth be told, formal and proper learning equips one with the power of expression in such a way that people won't find it difficult to understand what one is saying.

I have had to work so hard because I don't have the kind of education required to get a proper job. Life can truly be complicated for those who don't understand what life is about. Children who despise education, after have grown to a certain age and they come to know the importance of education, often realized they missed the opportunity of having a good education. If the life ahead of them is to be enjoyable, as against being miserable, they ought to be made to value education at a younger age. This fact is as natural as it is spiritual.

Furthermore, it is important to know how to conduct yourself and this is why it is necessary to acquire as much knowledge as you can get and be where you can do whatever you have got to do. It helps you carry on well in life. Failure to do this makes so many people get confused in life and then life seems not to be worth living. This is what happens to people that don't understand how to deal with the circumstances when they have created the problem themselves. I am saying this because I know what it is like to be disorganized because you do not have enough proper learning. People tend to look down on you; and when they do, you begin to think you are stupid while you are not. Frankly speaking, the pressure people put upon themselves sometimes are uncalled-for. Unknown to them, however, some of these things happen as a result of being hard-headed to the parent, teacher, and even those God has divinely placed along our paths to guide us through the journey of life; be it man, woman, boy or girl.

When I was a child, I didn't follow anyone's instruction because I thought that I knew enough to do what I needed to do. But, I found out later that there is nothing to be ashamed of when you acknowledge that you have not done what you should as long as you are ready to right the wrongs. The moment this is done, you are likely to realize that you are teachable. I am saying this because it hurts to see anyone get themselves into something that they might regret in the end. This is why it is important to listen and take instructions from one that knows more than you do. First of all, you need to know when the opportunity is right for instructions. But sometimes it's difficult to get the right direction if you're not well positioned. If you can't read, you sometimes have to depend on someone else in order to get instructions, but you have to know the person is giving you the right instruction. I guess I am struggling so hard today because I didn't position myself well at the earlier stages of my life. If I had done what I was supposed to do earlier in life, I would have been in better shape and so would my children.

As I went down through life, I didn't' take instructions from anyone nor from God, so I fell short in many things. I brought so much sorrow upon my own self. There is one thing I had in mind: encouraging those who won't give up. This is why I said to the Lord, "What can I do to help others?" He gave me instructions on what to do for other people. However, it was at 72 that I came to the understanding of how to help other people. I got myself into trouble being disobedient to man and God. Maybe I depended too much on the tools I called horses – the hoe and the rake. I work so people will know they can do something if they try. The point is that most people today are only interested in the short-cut to success. They don't want to suffer and this is reason there is so much killing, stealing, and raping and so many other vices. There is no short-cut to being responsible – being responsible involves taking responsibilities.

I have tried my best to put down where somebody can get instructions. In case you are wondering who this is, some people call me John Earl, Minister Harris, and Vegetable Man. Life can be sweet if a man can learn but they can't learn if they don't try. I didn't try until I came to be over 40; that was when it dawned on that I was not who I should be and had not achieved the things I ought to have achieved in life. Consequently, I became ashamed because I hadn't helped myself enough to help others. I was trying to hide because I was ashamed and this is why a lot of people are ashamed to let anyone know they don't know what they need to know. This shame sometimes leads to dope addiction and alcoholism. I am simply sharing with you the knowledge that came from what I have experienced.

April 22, 2004

A Letter from Satan

I saw you yesterday as you began your daily chores. You awoke without kneeling to pray. As a matter of fact, you didn't even bless your meals or prayed before going to bed last night. You are so unthankful. I like that about you. I cannot tell you how glad I am that you have not changed your way of living. Fool…, you are mine!!!

Remember, you and I have been going steady for years and I don't love you yet. As a matter of fact, I hate you. I hate you because I hate God. I'm only using you to get even with God. He kicked me out of heaven and I'm going to use you to pay HIM back for as long as possible. You see fool, God loves you and He has great plans in store for you, but you have yielded your life to me and I'm going to make your life a living hell. That way we'll be together twice. This will really hurt God. Thanks to you, I'm really showing HIM who's the boss of your life. With all the good times we had: watching dirty movies, cussing folks out, partying, stealing, lying, cheating, being a hypocrite, fornicating, overeating, smoking, drinking, playing hooky from church, telling dirty jokes, gossiping, backstabbing folks, and getting high…surely you don't want to give all this up? Come on fool, let's burn together forever! I've got some hot plans for us.

This is just a letter of appreciation from me to you. I'd like to say thanks for letting me use you for the most part of your life. Fool, you are so gullible. I laugh at you when you are tempted to sin and give in. HA! HA! HA! You even make me sick!!! Sin is beginning to take its toll on your life. You look twenty years older. I need some new blood. So go ahead, teach the little kids how to sin. All you have to do is: smoke, drink, cheat, gamble, gossip, fornicate, do drugs, cuss, over eat, miss Sunday School and week night services, party hearty, and listen and dance to the top ten jams. Do all of this in the presence of children and they will do it too. Kids are like that. Well fool, I've got to go now. I'll be back in a few seconds to tempt you again. If you were smart, you would run somewhere, confess your sins, and live for God with what little bit of life you have left. It's not my nature to warn anyone, but to be of your age and still sinning is becoming a bit ridiculous. Don't get me wrong. I still hate you! It's just that you'd make a better fool for Christ!!!

(If you really love me you will not share this letter.)

Look me up in the Holy Bible St. John 8:44

Confusion

Don't let confusion get you where you can't do what you need to do. I am saying this because I was once in those shoes. They were big shoes indeed. I got confused and I didn't know exactly what to do until I came to myself. Then I came to the conclusion that the way a man thinks a lot of times confuses him. He doesn't know what to do, but he is too proud-hearted to admit it and ask for help. He needs help but he doesn't seem to have the confidence in someone who could tell him what is right. I know what I am talking about because I used to be that way. I didn't trust anyone to tell me what the right thing to do was. I was afraid to trust anyone because I couldn't read or write. Simply put, I was vulnerable.

A man, woman, boy or girl needs to ask someone that has more experience in life for help. It was so hard for me to do what I needed to do until I met someone I could trust. I had to do a lot of unnecessary suffering because I was too suspicious of people. A person has to be mindful, particularly, about what they say and how they say it. There can be a lot of misunderstanding. If you must go far in life, you must not step on toes, especially the wrong toes. That is the more reason everyone seems to need someone to guide them through life. If you must be understood in life, you have to first be able to understand others.

People don't get enough instructions in life from people who have more experience. Societies, world over, have failed in the orientation of young minds; and in the real sense, a mind that is not oriented will be disoriented in the long run. Think about it, why are there so much crime in the world when criminality is not one of the moral ideals of any society? Children are not being taught when they are young about how to treat other people. It is hard for a child to understand these things alone. Once they are used to getting things done their own way, when they are grown, they live life their own way irrespective of what their society thinks or say. At that stage, they no longer listen to people who try to teach them. They try to outdo each other. When they cannot outwit the other person, they get mad. They destroy their inner vision and are driven by the things they see. I know what I am talking about because I used to be this way. Though I didn't get mad, I just always thought I could do anything that other people couldn't do.

I worked on my garden plot with a garden fork. I got where I could work a quarter of an acre each day. This is why I made up my mind not to be a bum and be a burden to anyone. I created my own problems and I had to find a way to solve them. I had to wash my clothes in a five gallon bucket in order not to be a burden on anyone. A man, woman, boy or girl needs to take responsibility for their own business. They need to be taught as a child to be responsible for themselves, and when they are grown, they will be responsible for their own problems and their own business. When I was a child, I was not taught to take responsibility for my own problems. I was only trained to work. When you are not taught as a child, you get confused. A man cannot take care of his family and take care of other business if he cannot take responsibilities. Many people will try to help. If you don't take heed to the one trying to help you, you will get into trouble. Most of the time, the average man will become a dope addict and the average woman will become a prostitute. Without mincing words, it is the responsibility of the older people to train the children and pass down the generational legacies passed down to them by their own parents and even grandparents. I hope someone will understand what I am talking about before it is too late. When children get to a certain age, it is difficult to train them. They need to be taught how they should conduct themselves and how they should treat one another before it is too late. What is happening is going to destroy a lot of people if they don't take heed to raise their children to behave themselves before others. This is the conclusion of this matter.

Don't Let Anything Destroy Your Mind

Don't let anything destroy your mind because you have done what you were not supposed to do. You still have to have the courage to keep going. There are things that you didn't do that you were supposed to do. Don't let the thought of it destroy your mind. I am saying what I'm saying because if it hadn't been for hope I wouldn't have been able to express myself, talking about what I should have done. What you can't change you must learn to accept. You have got to put it behind you and look forward to brighter days; because life can be miserable if you don't know how to cope with it.

Many people turn to dope and alcohol because they don't know how to cope with their problems. The truth remains that certain problems cannot be solved on your own. You need to sit down and listen to someone who has experienced the problem and can help you learn to cope with it. I know what it means and how it feels to be miserable. Trust me; it's not an ideal path for anyone. I have had some bad experiences because I was hard-headed and wouldn't listen to people who could have helped me. I thought I knew all I needed to know until I found out that in life there is always someone who can help you if you will let them assist you through their experiences.

Apart from learning from those who are more experienced and exposed than you are, you must also learn to be happy. However, true happiness won't come if you are always after immediate gains. Seeing the end of a thing from the beginning is the characteristic of man if have not fully harnessed. If you can't see the future right from the beginning, how do you help others? How do you get your children to see what life is all about? If you are not happy, life can be miserable. To be factual, one of the reasons people commit suicide is because they cannot cope with the problems of life without happiness.

The bottom line is that everyone has got to live with what they make of themselves. It's always a matter of choice. As you can choose to be happy, you can also choose to be miserable. I know this because I have been down the road. I am therefore trying all I could to help those who care to listen, with my little understanding and knowledge of life, to avoid such miserable experiences as I had. I have chosen to share my experiences via this medium because I felt more people would read through and it might have a better impact. If I were to narrate my story verbally, how many people would listen to an educated man like me? They might say within them that if he had that much knowledge why doesn't he have more than he does?

The true worth of a person is not in his material acquisition. Irrespective of whom you are or what you have, you need to appreciate the opportunity you have to instruct others, and do it each time as if there wouldn't be another time for it. If you had the opportunity to instruct children, it is important you teach them how to appreciate their mother and father. For the parents, children learn better and faster when they are instructed by someone who truly loves them. Teach them to love with love and they will learn to love their world. This is as far as I can go with the knowledge and understanding that came my way through experience.

John Harris,
APRIL 20, 2005

…Faith into Action

Living on the breath of faith has been my saving grace all this while. I had no better option than to live the life of faith. I was stripped down to a point where I had nowhere else to go; a point where I stumbled on faith and faith just never let me down. Seeing how important faith has become to my life, I had to put faith into action. As much as I tried to get someone to help me, they always seemed to have their own intentions. I started to wonder why people do not want to help other people. I was that desperation that led me to put faith into action. I wanted to see people helped in every way possible.

If you are not educated enough to put sentences together you might not get the kind of attention you desire from people; they might not even give you a chance to express yourself. Sometimes, they all think that you are stupid. I am emphasizing on the need to get formal education and be truly educated because I know painful it feels to be overlooked.

Sometimes, when I gave out my manuscripts to the people talking about education, they ignore me because they don't realize how important having education is to me. At such times, I wished I got education – the kind of education that would enable me express myself and get a good paying job. Education opens the way to the riches of the world; having it gives you access to have good cars and homes because you can have a good paying job. Frankly speaking, the world tends to push you aside if you can't read and write. Notwithstanding, you mustn't be discouraged. If you are too old to get education from the classrooms, you can get it through your interactions with those who are educated. The truth is that if your determination to succeed is strong enough, you can get success out of all you do. You might not get the kind of job you desire due to your being uneducated, but having educated friends can improve your chances of living a better life. Don't be discouraged.

Furthermore, it is important to know that only the responsible can put faith into action. How do others believe your stories when you are not responsible enough to admit your mistakes and make amends? How do they, when all you do is blame the world for you mistakes? Think about it, what kind of experience would you put on record for your children? Children learn more from the things they see and hear. One who is not responsible enough to take responsibilities is likely not to be able to teach the children how to be responsible. These children also begin to make a mess of their lives and in the end blame it on their parent. We should teach our children the way to go and how to relate peacefully with others while they are young and when they grow up in life, they find it easier to understand other people much better.

Imagine how children, who are used to seeing their parents quarrel, or drink and live on hard drugs, would relate with the world! They feel like everything and everybody is against them and want to do everything they can to outwit others. Sometimes they feel because they don't have the things that other children have they must destroy the other children to get it. When children don't get the kind of love they should get from their parents, teachers and everyone around them, they tend to struggle through life and in the process become a threat to their world. The reason some parents don't try to take care of their children is because they are dope addicts, prostitutes and the likes. Even if they tried to, their lifestyle will contradict what they say.

For those who still think they can't make anything good out of life, my message to them is simple: you are what you think. I took a shovel and hoe in order to till the land to produce food to sell and eat. My tools for survival have been shovel, hoe, garden fork, and rake. That is how faith is put into action. God will only bless what you have and not what you are looking forward to having. You can be a blessing to your world. Don't give up!

John Harris,
May 9, 2005

Lazy People Cause Troubles for Themselves

Laziness is not only a shameful act; it is an attitude that leads to failure. I wish people know how much hurt they cause themselves by being lazy. Lazy people shift their responsibilities to others, yet they always want to benefit from others' hard work. The truth remains that it will be very difficult for a lazy person to be honest; and honesty is what it takes to build a long lasting relationship with others. I have had to live without a lot of things trying to be honest and truthful to people because I want people to be honest and truthful with me. In all, I did what I did to avoid being a burden on someone else. I have washed my clothes in a five gallon bucket because I didn't want to be a burden. I knew I made it hard for myself by not taking heed to my mother, father, and the ones that were showing me that certain things would happen if I didn't do certain things. I thought it was just a fairy tale because I thought they were just against me. Now I am taking responsibilities for my past actions because it was my fault entirely. I am always eager to share my experiences with someone else while they have a chance to enjoy life. I didn't really know what life is all about until I came to be of a certain age and God called me into the ministry.

Not taking responsibilities can crumble marriages and even ministries. Marriages are breaking easily today because it is difficult for a man or a woman to give up certain aspects of their lives in order to live with others – they always want to have things done their own way. Consequently, each of them gives up their responsibility as wife or husband. When this happens, the children are affected the most. Parents who are not responsible cannot teach their children how to be responsible. This might sound harsh, but it's the truth: God will hold parents accountable for failing their children.

Laziness is often the cause of irresponsibility. Some have deprived themselves of getting educated as a result of their laziness. The truth about laziness is that it doesn't begin at adulthood. It is more of a habit that has accumulated overtime. However, it is hard to make a decent living unless you have a decent education. A lazy person is always on the lookout, trying to take advantage of those working hard because they are too sorry to help themselves. They play tricks, schemes, and all sorts of games trying to get something for nothing. The beautiful things about life is that whether you get it right or wrong, there is always an end result; this is what we call consequences. I have tried many things but it would not work because it wasn't right. Taking something that doesn't belong to you will cause you to suffer in future. The bottom-line is that a lazy person brings destruction on his own self.

John Harris
August 10, 2005

The Fork and the Shovel

Starting in 2003, I used the fork and the shovel because the ground was so hard. I used the pick to get the ground pulverized so I could plant the seed. I had enough faith and confidence in myself that I wasn't going to give up because I didn't have the proper learning to get a proper job. So, I kept one thing in mind: Where there is a will, there is a way. I didn't give up and that was what kept me going. I was trying to show the people what you can do if you tried. People might discourage you in so many ways; they might laugh and make mockery of your vision, yet, you afford to give up on your dreams. Many never thought I could write this book. When I told them what I had in mind to do, they laughed at the idea and made fun of me; but I knew that where there is a will, there will always be a way. My story isn't a fairy tale; it is reality – a reality I wish to share with others in order to encourage and inspire them. Never you give up!

Don't Cut Off the Hand That Feeds the Mouth

You can't climb to the top all on your own; you would need people to help you get there. Some will help you willingly, others might make demands. Whichever way it turns out, when you get to the top, don't cut off the hand that feeds your mouth. Better put, don't bite the fingers that feed you. When people help you in any way, courtesy demands that you acknowledge their inputs. They might not ask for it; they might not even need it, nevertheless, you still must give honour to those who deserve it.

Think of it this way: those who help you on your way to the top are like ladder-rungs who take you up and could bring you back down when you need them to. But, when push off the ladder after you got to the top, it won't be there when you need it the most. Some of such people are the teachers.

If teachers are remembered and appreciated by all the students they have taught, they should rank amongst the wealthiest in the world. Teachers are the hands that feed the society at large; they are the ones who feed the nation's economy with professionals from all walks of life, yet, they most often struggle to survive. Aside from remembering and appreciating them at later times, they should be obeyed and respected. Failure to do so is like cutting off the hand that feeds you. Notwithstanding, it takes those who understand the value of education to worship the teachers. The point being made here is that irrespective of the social status those who facilitate you getting to the top; you must not ignore them even when it is obvious that you are way beyond their levels.

Many times I have done without food trying to help others. Then they thought they were taking advantage of me because they thought I was old and didn't know what I was saying and doing. I suffered to make it better for others because I know what it is like to be pushed aside for lack of education. I am sharing my experience in a bid to help others avoid getting hurt. As untrue as it may sound, sometimes some people give up on survival because they have been hurt by their loved ones. Nevertheless, no matter how discouraging life may look, you must carry on regardless of what somebody says and does to you. You are responsible for what you do and the way you conduct your life.

John Harris
October 10, 2005

The Computer Can Be Dangerous

The computer can be dangerous if you don't use it wisely. This is what is destroying so many of our young teenagers. They don't teach them to use it wisely. This is what came to my mind. I was seeing how the young people destroy themselves because they have not been taught the dangers of the internet. This is why the person with no education or experience can get caught up in the thing. They are not aware of the dangers. The activities of the young ones on the internet should be monitored; that way, the adults can see what they are doing on the internet and teach them to be wise. It is destroying the people because they are not taught to use it wisely.

The Dangers of Dope

Many often think that "Doping" is something that can help a person if they use it wisely. This is what destroys the young people because they are not taught to use it wisely. It is good if it is used for what it was made for. A lot of people don't use it wisely and don't pass it on to other people how to use it wisely. The older generation needs to pass on to the younger generation how to use it wisely. This is what is destroying the young people. The older people don't have enough concern for one another. We see our neighbors in need and we withdraw because of what someone might say or do. We need not care about what people think. We need to help one another to use these things for what they were made for. Everything God made is good if it is used correctly. This is what came to me about what is going on. Things take place in people's lives that make them miserable and they feel like everything is not worth living. They don't know what life is all about and they think someone should do everything for them. They think their time is more valuable than other people's time. This is what causes confusion among the nation because one person thinks everyone should do things his way. They need to be taught that what is fair for one is fair for the other. If you don't have enough knowledge or experience, life can be awfully miserable.

The Power of Prayer

When a person is stripped down to nothing but prayer and faith, then he has to pray himself out and depend on the knowledge and the understanding of how to build their confidence up by themselves. I have come to learned one thing in life; if you don't give up your hope, you can have something better. This is why I try my best to be a living testimony for somebody else so they can see what the power of prayer can do. There was a lady that could not walk. We prayed for her and prayer helped her to walk again. Her name is Sally Jones. There was another lady who had a tree she wanted someone to cut out of her yard. It was set on fire. This is why I know prayer does work. I had kidney problems and prayer healed my body. I had hemorrhoids and prayer healed me. This is why I know what prayer can do. I was out in my field one day and I was so tired I thought I could not go on. I prayed and asked God for strength and my legs felt like a brand new pair of legs. I know beyond any doubts that prayer works.

The Coming Drought

It is time for people to stop wasting their food because it's going to be scarce and this is what came to me. I was in the field and I thought about Joseph when famine was in the land. I tried my best to understand what it was saying. The only thing that I could understand was the drought. They aren't going to be able to buy because there is going to be a famine and this is why I am trying to let people know that God always warns us through people. This is why I am trying to get people to understand but it is hard to understand that a man that can't read or write can tell them anything reasonable. They feel he can't be used to get the program over to help people because they feel like a person that don't have as much material things can't tell them anything. They feel like he doesn't know what he is talking about. I thought about when Joseph was in Egypt. I tried to figure out what it was all about but every time that He gave me a vision I try to warn the people so they will not get caught up in something they will regret in the future. It looks like to them that God can't use me but I let them know that the least person there is can be used; but God only speaks through the humble. This is why I try to encourage others as I go along. I try to warn the people because the word of God is going to be fulfilled.

So, this is what came to my mind about the drought. It took some time to understand what was going on in my mind. Sometimes, I think I am losing my mind because I don't understand many things but I try to pray to God to give me understanding so I can pass it along to others. They try their best to make it hard for a person with no education. They feel like they have to look up to them for help but we all need some encouragement. No matter how old you are or how much you have, you still need encouragement from others. I warn you through what I have learned by being hardheaded and contrary. I am so glad that I didn't get to a point where I gave up hope. As long as you have hope there is a change to do better. When you lose hope there is no hope.

Most people were saying about the drought that they were not planting until the rains come. Now I can see the value of planting before the rain. I continued to plant and when the rain came my crops came up. When you are wise, you can survive no matter how tough things get.

John Harris
August 3, 2006

Don't Give Up, There Is Hope!

This is what came to me while I was in the field. Something spoke to me and said "Don't give up. This is hope." I started planting in the dirt and it was so dry until I had to plant it in the dirt but something kept encouraging my heart to keep on going because everything will be alright someday. I went ahead and planted all I could. I planted peas, okra, tomatoes, sweet potatoes, and string beans. The people asked me how it was all going to grow when it was so dry. I told them that you have to believe that it's going to rain someday. Then it started raining and most of the seeds came up. Some I had to plant again but I wasn't going to give up. Now I can see the harvest because I didn't give up. .There is always hope if you don't give up.

Some people have cancer or other illness but you have to fight in order to stay alive. When you give up there is no hope but there is always hope if you don't give up. It depends on each and every individual to believe they can make it. The average person if they aren't careful and mindful will give up because when they get old it feels like there is no hope. This is why I try to encourage others not to give up. There is a way out. It only gets complicated because you cannot see the future. The future lies in the hands of God. This is why I had enough faith not to give up. People were laughing at me and saying, "You are working for nothing," but something kept encouraging me. I would get up at two and three in the morning and go to the filed. It was so hot I would change shirts four and five times a day. I did not give up because I could see the result and the joy of having what I planted.

This is why you have to keep faith and trust in what you are doing; if you don't it might be hard for a person to see the future. This is why I tell the young people, you have to work for the future. People want someone to crack the hickory nut and get the goody out and give it to them. They don't want to suffer to get what they need. I worked out in the heat and they want me to give them some of my harvest.

People don't want to do the work themselves, yet they want to get every bit of the benefits attached to work. When you don't understand the future, life can be miserable. Old people don't teach the young people to be responsible. And this is the power of the hickory nut. Old people used to use parables to teach young people responsibility. If you have never had cancer or sickness, you don't know what the other person is going through. So you should be lovely and kind to everyone, because you don't know what the other person is going through. To each person will come a time of sorrow. If you are not prepared, you will give up hope. You will feel like life is not worth living.

John Harris
September 21, 2006

Don't Destroy Yourself

While I was in the field, I was disturbed because people were taking my vegetables and I thought of ways to get back at them. But something came to my mind warning me not to try to get even with others. This is why so much happens to other people. They often listen to what others say or do that they end up destroying themselves. And then when I heard this voice I had to laugh at myself; because I was tempted to throw back at the people that were doing me wrong. But I learned that wouldn't solve the problem. The things that I do, I am responsible for. And this is why a lot of people do not think before they do things. Each and every person is responsible for what they do and say. If you listened to the wrong source calling you to get into something evil, you might regret it in the future.

This is the problem with husband and wife who throw back on each other for what they do. They don't understand that they are responsible for what they do and say. When they listen to the wrong voice, they do things that they regret in the future. When all this came to my mind I said "Thank you for all you gave to me."

When I tell people all these things, they think I have made them all up. But it has been given to me by the Lord; because he always warns people. I look around at all the people who have education and don't use it wisely. It causes them to get into trouble because they won't take heed to what they have learned. It is no good to know what is right and not do it. This is why they bring so much destruction on themselves.

John Harris
November 20, 2006

The Importance of Music

Something was dropped in my mind about music:

Now, music can be dangerous to the person's mind if it is the wrong music. This is what came to my mind about music. If a person listens to the wrong music it will mess up their mind. It will make them do foolish things because the music will control the person's mind. Music often soothes the mind but if they don't have the right attitude toward the music, it will mess up their mind. It came to me that this is why so many people are destroying each other and themselves when they are under the influence of alcohol or dope or any strong drink. When they are under the influence of music, it will cause them to destroy themselves and other people because music plays a big part in a person's life. Music started in the Bible when David was playing the harp. Music is important to God; it makes the difference in the lives of those who know how to handle it.

As wonderful as the sound of music is, it can wreak havoc on humanity if not properly used. People will be riding along listening to music and talking on the telephone. All of a sudden, the inevitable happens. This is because music could be so captivating and sometimes distractive. God wants people to be aware of these things. Music is so important that men that train horses or other animals, even snakes, take music into training them. Music plays a vital role in a person's life. It helps to lift the soul when the spirit is down; it is also inspiring and therapeutic. However, music can be both encouraging and damaging, depending on how it is used.

A lot of people don't believe this but music is the spirit of the universe. It is destroying a lot of young ones today. Music is causing them to do many foolish things especially when they are under the influence of alcohol and drugs. Music makes them destroy their friends, loved ones and themselves because they don't know its effect on the human psychic. We should learn to believe in the power of music and begin to use it to the benefit of the human race.

From Every Sin

"He shall save his people from their sins."

---Matthew 1:21

LORD, save me from my sins. By the name of Jesus, I am encouraged thus to pray. Save me from my past sins, that the habit of them may not hold me captive. Save me from my constitutional sins, that I may not be the slave of my own weaknesses. Save me from the sins which are continually under my eye that I may not lose my horror of them. Save me from secret sins … sins unperceived by me from my want of light. Save me from sudden and surprising sins: let me not be carried off my feet by a rush of temptation. Save me, Lord, from every sin. Let not any iniquity have dominion over me.

Thou alone canst do this. I cannot snap my own chains or slay my own enemies. Thou knowest temptation, for thou wast tempted. Thou knowest sin, for thou didst bear the weight of it. Thou knowest how to succor me in my hour of conflict; thou canst save me from sinning and save me when I have sinned. It is promised in thy very name that thou wilts do this, and I pray thee let me this day verify the prophecy. Let me not give way to temper, or pride, or despondency, or any form of evil; but do thou save me unto holiness of life, that the name of Jesus may be glorified in me abundantly.

Appendix

3

Revelations

My Testimony

My wife and I were separated and I had to go back home where I had said I would never go back to. I thank my mother for letting me stay in her old trailer. When I first moved in, I didn't have anything on – nothing like lights, water or heat and it was winter time. I didn't have anything but clothes and the trailer was so cold and it needed some work on it. So I had to stay in one room with no heat or food for a couple of days. My sister helped me out a whole lot. She gave me a heater and some food every day. I want to thank her for helping out poor me. And then it got worst; my car was taken away from me. I didn't know what to do. I didn't have any money to fix it and I had already borrowed money from my boss man. I had some old fines that I had to pay or else they were going to pick me up. I was in a mess. So, I finally found myself a way to work every day. But I had to walk about two miles each morning and evening to my house and some mornings it was very cold.

Sometimes it was so cold that I couldn't feel my hands and sometimes it rained on me. I remember one Friday I had to walk two miles home with three heavy bags but I refused to give up. I said, "God you got to do something, I am tired of walking." Please fix it so that I won't have to walk any more. Now, I still don't have a car but I have a way to work. I don't want to walk anymore." I thank the Lord for fixing it just for me.

But I still wasn't satisfied because I was living uncomfortably in a room with no water, bathroom, and the trailer was still cold. I felt so bad that I wanted to lie down and die. I would fall on my knee and pray hard.

I told the Lord, "I'm tired of living this way." I know, Lord, that I put myself in this mess but I need you to help me out of this. I will make you a promise that I will start honoring your commandments and do whatever it takes to please you because my life is over. One night, a voice came to me and said go out there and repair your own trailer. My trailer sat behind my mother's trailer and it needed a lot of work. I started to think about doing the work but at the time I needed a car. Again, a voice came to me and spoke to me and said, "I know the trouble that you are in; I made you." If you had a car, you will let the devil fool you. You will start having misunderstanding with your wife again and this is why I am not giving you a car. So, please obey me; go out there and start working on your trailer. You are to work on it every day after work. I never looked back; it took me ten months to finish but I repaired my own trailer. It cost me approximately five thousand dollars to remodel. However, I went from living in one room to a three bedroom with one bathroom trailer and it was all paid for. God gave me a chance to turn my life around and I now have a paradise here on earth. I was headed for death but God had mercy on me.

This Is the Mystery of What the Lord Has Showed Me about Different Things

I wanted to record my revelations in written form that others might be able to read them. I want people to understand life and its misery and mystery. When my mother was trying to tell me about life, I never thought it was something that was worth hearing. But now that I am older, I can tell young people that what your parents are trying to tell you is worth hearing. They are sharing from their experiences.

As I grew, the more I experienced and understood. There are some things in life that are factual. It will occur whether you are rich, poor, black or white. Thus, believe it or not … what you do as a child you will see it again. You might be middle aged or retired but your inappropriate behavior will catch up with you before you die.

At the time that you are putting illegal substances into your body, it seems right and feels good at such moments. However, at some point in your life, your body will remind you of your abusive and destructive habits. This is why parents should warn their children about using drugs and alcohol.

God revealed to me that I was to share this message with the people of my community. I want to see people enjoying life and being successful in life. But, if we fail to warn people and our youth about the deception that lies in their paths, they won't make it. Sometimes, our youth are narrow minded, unconcerned, and have the "I don't care attitude". In these instances, they don't try to help themselves or others.

My mother would tell me that life was what you made it out to be. I found out that life was not a fairy tale. And what she shared with me was true because every time I did something contrary to her teaching, I suffered the unwanted consequence. I learned the hard way that to go against knowledge wasn't a joke. As a minister, I do my best to share with people the lessons that I have learned. I share with boys and girls that enjoyment of life often depends upon how you treat other people.

The love that we share with others makes a difference in life. Yet, we have to be careful because narrow-minded people will try to take advantage of people who share love. Though it is saddening but true; these people believe that what they do is right. Therefore, live a life that demonstrates love but be careful of narrow-minded and selfish people. Such people often envy other people's position and status in life.

Education makes a difference in life, but mothers play the biggest role in shaping a child's future. Education does many things for persons but only mothers can teach love and wisdom. However, understanding God's word can do more than education or a mother. Obedience to God's word is a must if we truly wish to enjoy life.

Revelation about Reform Temple Church

I, John Earl Harris, was the first deacon of the *Reform Temple Church*. I was the first preacher of the Reform Church. Something disturbing occurred in the church and this was shown to me. I didn't understand until the church moved to another place and changed its name. The first Reform Temple is now Reform Community Church. Now, when the churches have their church's anniversary, they will know their history.

The place called Poplar Springs is where Reform Temple had its beginning. It is now in Reform, Alabama. Poplar Springs gets its name from a spring that was under a Poplar tree. I wanted to record this so people can know their history. The record will show that I was the first deacon and preacher of Reform Temple. Also, I was the first preacher of the Church of God in Christ of Poplar Springs. This is the conclusion on Reform Temple.

Hughes Town:

The first name given to Hughes town's church was Hughes Temple. I, John Earl Harris, was the first preacher of the church. God told me to tell the people about the founding of Hughes Temple. He told me to keep the church going and not to let it dissolve. He told me to tell the people to cherish what God gives. God gave this revelation to share the founding of Hughes Temple because sometimes people attempt to take credit for what they did not do. On the other hand, sometimes people don't know what they need to know. God does not give a revelation for the purpose of hiding it but that it might be shared.

For me to share this revelation, I have had to seek the help of many persons. I have had to ask many questions. Because I cannot read or write, sometimes it was difficult for people to understand my questions. On many occasions, people became irritated by me. But, I made every effort to get my revelations on paper. I knew that people would think that I was a lunatic if I did get my revelations on paper; especially the young people. For some people, they would rather read about something else than listen to a person trying to explain mysteries of life. This is the wisdom of my revelation. This is the conclusion of the matter.

www.ingramcontent.com/pod-product-compliance
Lightning Source LLC
Chambersburg PA
CBHW070546300426
44113CB00011B/1809